GO DOWN
TO THE
POTTER'S HOUSE

GO DOWN
TO THE
POTTER'S HOUSE

A JOURNEY
INTO MEDITATION

Donagh O'Shea OP

DOMINICAN PUBLICATIONS

First published (1988) by
Michael Glazier, Inc. and Dominican Publications

This revised edition published (2013) by
Dominican Publications
42 Parnell Square
Dublin 1

ISBN 978-1-905604-25-8

British Library Cataloguing in Publications Data.
A catalogue record for this book is available
from the British Library.

Origination by Dominican Publications
Cover design by Bill Bolger and Susan Waine
Cover photograph by Donagh O'Shea

Printed in Ireland by
SPRINT-print
Rathcoole
Co. Dublin

Contents

Introduction

The deeper the valleys, the loftier the heights that rise above them; the deeper the well, the higher too: for depth and height are the same thing.

   Meister Eckhart

The newspapers I found in the attic were from the 1890s, and their language was more florid than any we would use today except in jest. When they praised a new book or a speech, they said it was full of *lofty thoughts* or *elevated sentiments.* As I sat among the dust-laden leavings of the past I meditated on the passage of time – the most pathetic mystery, the sum of all pities. Enthusiasms, passions, projects: all turn to dust and silence. Attics are for such moody meditations, and few of us could endure them for longer than an hour or two.

   As I came down from the attic I wondered what words we might use in place of *lofty* and *elevated.* It struck me with great force that we would use precisely the opposite words: *deep, profound.* Language often turns on its heel in this way, and we have to use the opposite words to say the same thing.

   Linguistic changes reflect other changes – social, cultural, religious. For example, strongly hierarchical societies found it natural to pray, "Glory to God in the highest," but it would chime better with our spirit if we prayed, "Glory to God in the deepest." Depth and height, Meister Eckhart assured us, are the same thing; but metaphors of depth speak more intimately to us than metaphors of height.

   If a Christian of today finds an air of unreality about religious language, it may not be due to a lack of faith but to the difficulty of taking in "lofty", untranslated concepts which have no *body* in experience. Great energy is released when a truth is experienced in a full-bodied way; and the Christian faith is nothing if not full-bodied: Jesus is the Word made flesh. He is God's body language. But in our practice we reverse this and we turn everything into words. One would think that the central revelation was, "the flesh was made word."

For example, we have made the physical elements of the sacraments so tenuous that they are not really signs any more but only ciphers. The baptismal triple immersion became attenuated to a small dribble on the head; massaging with oil became a tiny smear with one thumb; the presence of confessor to penitent became so veiled that he was only a voice; the bread of the Eucharist is only the *idea* of bread, weightless and two-dimensional. It would not be correct to attribute this development to convenience alone, because great inconvenience was the mark of most other things that we did in the Church. More likely, it was due to a persuasion that the spiritual life was not about the body but only about the mind and soul. The physical elements of the sacraments then shed their own reality as fullbodied signs and began to operate as mere signals, triggering grace in the soul. An abstract distinction between the natural and the supernatural (especially when it was not seen for an abstraction) seemed to bless this decline and make it self-evident.

The background to our present complex age is four centuries of introspection and individualism. But perhaps we are already shedding some of the crippling weight of this inheritance and discovering in ourselves a straightforward simplicity that we thought had vanished from the earth.

This book is the story of the Mews, which is part of St Dominic's Retreat Centre in Cork. The old buildings of the Mews are a perfect site for the pottery workshop, the meditation centre and the Hermitage. Here we have retreats under the general heading, *The Body in Prayer.* These retreats have evolved as methods of full-bodied prayer and palpable ways of seeking God. They are in continuity with the spiritual tradition of the Order in which I have spent more than half my life. It is often true that the nearer something is, the harder it is to see. It is only in recent years that I have taken notice of the thirteenth century writing called *On the Nine Ways of Prayer of Saint Dominic.* It is a brief and beautiful text, and the coloured illustrations that go with it are masterpieces in their own right. It places a special emphasis on bodily prayer, each "way" being visible in a distinctive body-posture. Dominic's devotion "showed quite plainly in his bodily members ... the soul stirring the body and the body in turn stirring the soul" His prayer came from the whole self; and his preaching had the same stamp: according to Humbert of Romans it abounded in stories, metaphors and other "bodily ideas". The present book is a modest attempt to follow a similar course.

Centre and Periphery

It is certain that
if God is to be born in the soul
it must turn back to eternity …
must recall itself,
and concentrate all its faculties within itself,
the lowest as well as the highest.
All its dissipated powers
must be gathered up into one,
because unity is strength.
John Tauler

The clay is running true under the hands. When it centres itself there is a stillness. It is one of the most satisfying moments in the making of pottery. There is a comforting smoothness and vitality in centred clay. It is the moment of possibilities, the silence before speech.

The speed and simplicity are deceptive. The struggle that now takes a few seconds once took many weeks. I learned the trade years ago in Prinknash Abbey. The monks allowed me to share their life and work for a time. Learning to be a potter may well seem an eccentric part for a priest, but in reality it was hardly more eccentric than the academic life I had been pursuing for years. "Eccentric" means "off-centre," but it was precisely a kind of personal centring that I was to find through working with clay.

Two things brought me to Prinknash. There was the moment, a year before, when for the first time I saw a potter working at the wheel and knew, with a certainty I have had about few things, that I had to become a potter. And there was the hunch that this work could put into focus some things that I had no satisfying words for. The rhythm of a full monastic life was a perfect setting for this kind of exploration. Rising at five is not as heroic as it seems, if you have had your seven hours. The body soon adjusts itself, and those early hours become the most perfect part of the day. The long Morning Office made the thought of porridge attractive for the first time in my life; but it also gave a sense of grandeur and solidity.

After porridge, clay. On my first morning in the pottery the monk in charge gave me a bag of it, directed me to a wheel and vanished. Thus began a month-long lonely struggle to learn the art of centring a lump of clay on the potter's wheel.

It can be said in one sentence: Grasp the spinning lump of clay between the hands, applying pressure from both sides until it no longer wobbles but runs true. Doing it, however, is a different story. Never was the difference between theory and practice so pitilessly clear.

The clay seemed to have a definite view of its own about centring: it preferred all other places to the centre. The wobble would sometimes grow less, as I squeezed with all my might, but soon it would renew itself, and even provide variations of rhythm that were especially irritating. There were moments when I was ready to believe that it was making fun of me as it moved from a syncopated to a two-sided wobble. Sometimes the quarrel between us became so intense that the lump detached itself completely from the wheel-head, as if to discourage any further effort. Even one day of this is enough to undermine the sturdiest self-confidence.

The situation was not helped by the glass wall through which tourists were able to view procedures in the workshop. There is nothing more humiliating, or more frightening, than to be gazed at out of curiosity by people who are not forming community with you. It is an abstract, passionless gaze. I experienced in the flesh what Kierkegaard meant by 'The Public': "that abstract whole formed by all the participants becoming a third party, an onlooker … this gallery on the lookout for distraction." Add some Kafka to convey the sense of threat. There was also the painful fact that I was the sole object under their gaze, for I was the only one working at the wheel; the others were making pots by the slip-casting method, in which there is nothing to distract even someone on the lookout for distraction. Such a public would never kill you out of hate, I kept thinking; they would dismember you out of curiosity. Or so it seemed, on my side of the glass. In reality I was the one reducing them to an abstraction. Because of the glass it was impossible to engage them humanly and explain that I was just a beginner. They seemed like cold pagan gods gazing on the human predicament.

Day by day, under the eye of The Public, I struggled forlornly with those lumps of clay, so unreasonably set in their ways. Then came a breakthrough: I had a clear realization that it is not with the hands alone that clay is centred; the forearms are needed. Anchoring these solidly on the tray that surrounds the wheel-head, I experienced a certain authority over the clay. This was more imagined than real, however, as the evil wobble soon proved. And yet a feeling of confidence is not nothing. Soon there was another breakthrough: a realisation that the entire arm and the shoulders have to come into play. The shoulders should be forward in a strong, dominating posture. This may have impressed The Public but, sadly, it had no effect at all on the clay.

Several days later I began to pay attention to the way I was sitting at the wheel. Backward and forward adjustments changed the whole 'feel' of the work. There was one position that had a feeling of rightness about it. Still the clay led its independent life. Later again I began to adjust the position of my feet on the floor. These exert pressures that we are seldom aware of but which affect everything we do. But still the clay refused to centre itself and run true.

If you have not struggled with whirling clay it is difficult to imagine how dispiriting an experience it is for the beginner. If it had not been for the sanity of monastic life I would probably not have persevered. Work is part of the rhythm of monastic life, but it is not the monk's reason for living. However interesting or important the work, it is put aside when it is time for prayer. This I found frustrating at first, since I am inclined to be a bit obsessive in my interests. If the pattern of the monastic day seems a little impersonal, it is because it does not follow the obsessions that drive us like moths into the flame. It is "long wisdom," not following human nerves but the pulse of God's life. When a mellower wisdom is all around you it is difficult to remain untouched by it. Stabilised, no doubt, by this (and porridge) I entered the pottery one morning and began effortlessly to centre large lumps of clay on the wheel.

The exhilaration of this went straight to the head and made me quite giddy for a time. The most puzzling aspect was the effortlessness. The lumps of clay seemed to centre themselves without my help. My 'help,' of course, meant that impatient running amuck that The Public had come to expect of me. How could so much energy fail to produce a result, and so little energy succeed? It called for reflection.

The monastery farm had numberless places that might have been specially designed for reflection: chestnut trees that had a kind of grandfatherly atmosphere under them, a duck-pond, an old forge worked by a monk of such transparent holiness that being with him was strangely like being alone, only much better. There was the farmyard with its earthy smells and its own pace. But of course there were also countless fences to sit on.

Sitting on one of these fences one evening, I had a sudden revelation. I call it that, though a lesser word might be more suitable. The moment of understanding is surely a kind of revelation, an opening of the mind. I saw with sudden clarity that what I had really been trying to do during the previous weeks was not just to centre the clay but to centre *myself*. The clay had drawn my body, inch by inch, into the task: first the hands, then the arms, later the shoulders, and the trunk, and eventually even the feet. When there was no more body to be drawn in, it drew in the mind (it was on a morning when the mind was at great peace that the miracle had happened).

The whole body and mind working together: that was a more profound centring than the centring of the clay, The clay was the outer shape, the indicator, of the inner centring. When I was centred – that is, acting as one force rather than as a cluster of contradictory ones – the clay showed this by its own centring, as it had so graphically shown the opposite before.

There was plenty of time in the monastery to unfold the revelation. I began to understand that the inner and outer worlds are not such that we can afford to have a preference for one over the other. They manifest each other in the minutest detail: what happens in one is immediately echoed in the other. A distinction became clear: between *introspection* and *interiority*. Though they look alike, they are quite opposite to each other. Introspection means living from the outside in; interiority, from the inside out.

> A small bird flew before me…
> He thought that I was after him for a feather
> The white one in his tail: like one who takes
> Everything said as personal to himself.
>   Robert Frost

That was an introspective bird. Interiority, on the other hand, is out-going, but it puts a deep personal stamp on everything one does. I read again some pages of the kindly fourteenth century mystic, John Tauler, looking carefully at each word: *turn back, recall, concentrate, gather up.* This was not neurotic introspection but a personal centring. I knew in my mind and body what he meant by dissipated powers that must be gathered up into one. And it was clear that the gathering up was not flight from the outer world. Potters at the wheel do not stop at feeling centred; they go ahead and make pots. Nor is the centring something that is done once and for all; one moment of forgetfulness destroys the outer work. It was as if the kindly counsellor were at my side, in the flesh.

His words echoed those of another kindly confrere who had said to me in a time of crisis: "If you want to help others, work on yourself." I was now translating this into my new language: "The way to centre the clay is to centre yourself." But more important was the retranslation from pottery back to ministry. My greatest outer mistakes came from inner wobbles; and my old solution (to work even harder) was like trying to centre the lump of clay by adding to it, or by unskilful force.

Next day I surveyed The Public with fresh enthusiasm, only to be met with the same glassy stare through the glass wall. I remembered with a start that I myself had been on their side, peering through that same glass wall on my first day at the abbey. How conveniently I had forgotten that! We never think of ourselves as the public, or as the man in the street, or as the average housewife. The public may be a faceless crowd, but it is only *as a crowd* that it is faceless. Each one there is a private person, protecting his or her privacy perhaps too well. What makes them a crowd is not only the way they look at me, but even more the way I look back at them. On a sudden inspiration I hurried to the office, made a large L-plate and fixed it to the frame of the wheel. I was rewarded with an array of warm smiles. What pain it would have saved me a few weeks before!

The effortless effort continued on the wheel. The meaning of much that I had read became clear to me day by day: that the most perfect actions are effortless.

> The wild geese do not intend to cast their reflection;
> The water has no mind to receive their image.
>   The Zenrin

Much of our energy is sidetracked by an awkward crossing of purposes within ourselves. The greatest obstacles are seldom in the outer world; they are within the self when there is a lack of clarity and integration. In fact, effortlessness is the mark of every skill. I had learnt well that skill is not merely physical achievement, and I remembered with pleasure that the Greeks called virtue *arete,* a word that meant *skill.* Then Meister Eckhart, Tauler's teacher, added this:

> When one can do the works of virtue without preparation, by willing to do them, and bring to completion some great and righteous matter without giving it a thought – when the deed of virtue seems to happen by itself, simply because one loved goodness and for no other reason, then one is perfectly virtuous and not before.

Learning this through the medium of pottery was a safeguard against expecting effortlessness at the beginning – a strong temptation in an age of instant effects. Eckhart constantly talked of God's effortlessness: "God loves to work," "God is full of enjoyment " The sun, he said, sheds its rays effortlessly; they are absorbed by everything, and yet the sun does not lose its radiance. Easy for God, I reflect. But were we not commanded to be perfect as our heavenly Father is perfect?

The worst enemy is humdrum philosophy, a vision that fails to do us justice. If virtue is always a grim struggle, how can there be any joy – except in vice? An old distrusted friend, the terrible and wonderful Nietzsche, came to my aid with the right word.

> What destroys more quickly than to work, to think, to feel without inner necessity, without a deep personal choice, without joy? as an automaton of duty?

If I do not grow up spiritually, virtue will continue to mean "what others want of me," and so vice will be identified with "what I want myself." This is how life becomes a guilt-ridden burden. For survival we flee to a separate, secret, inner place where we cannot be found out. This place then drains guilt into itself from every side and becomes full of confusion and insecurity.

It was a great pleasure to think that I was studying virtue as I enjoyed life in the pottery. For a work of virtue it was a very mucky business. I wondered if it wasn't this very aspect of it that created a sense of community among the potters. Surprisingly there were only two monks there; the rest were lay men and women. They were quite friendly in the way that very engrossed people are friendly: they talked only intermittently and sideways. There was a tangible sense of comradeship, and I was sure (at least for the time being) that this was healthier than the head-on sharing that people sometimes feel obliged to do. The potter beside me was a pleasant Jewish man named Paul, who smiled into his pot when I renamed him Saul.

The story of one's first pots is best left in obscurity. The worst temptation is to keep any of them. They are a chronicle in clay of all the weak vices: uncertainty, feebleness, hesitation, fussiness, lack of control, and a timidity sometimes bordering on pure funk. The Public, now disarmed by my L-plate, were kind enough to pass unseeing eyes over those still-born monsters. Nor was I cast down by this infanthood, for I had been granted some understanding of the path before me.

I was gratified, before leaving the Abbey, to come across a poem by Goethe (who was not considerate enough to write in English!) which expressed the kind of thoughts that became signposts along the path. First, a translation: Now turn your attention inwards: / You will find the Centre within.... / Then you must trust your senses, / They will show you nothing false / If your intelligence keeps you alert.)

> *Sofort nun wende dich nach innen*
> *Das Zentrum findest du da drinnen....*
> *Den Sinnen hast du dann zu trauen,*
> *Kein Falsches lassen sie dich schauen,*
> *Wenn dein Verstand dich wach erhalt.*

Concealment and Manifestation

With every creature, according to the nobility of its nature, the more it indwells in itself the more it gives itself out. Nothing has such a great sallying-forth as the soul in her highest part.

Meister Eckhart

Home has been called "a world of strife shut out, a world of peace shut in." This division is less certain when your home is a Retreat Centre that opens its doors to bus and carloads of strife every day. St Dominic's, Ennismore, my home for eight years, has been doing this for more than thirty years. Yet it manages, because of its seclusion and because a religious community lives there, to be a world of peace shut in.

On returning to Ireland from Prinknash Abbey in 1978 I was asked to join this community and devote my energy to giving retreats. About seven thousand people make retreats here every year, some groups staying for a single day, some for two days or a weekend, some for a week or longer. It is a privileged way for a priest to spend his years, for there is no need in such a place for small-talk: those who come here are not just passing the time, they are asking you a question, they are seekers.

S HE WANTED him to find God. Religion was the only difference between them; otherwise they were suited to each other, she said. They were getting engaged at Christmas and it would be nice if they could see eye to eye on this. They often had arguments about it and it would be a bad prospect for their marriage if these arguments continued. We sat, a company of three, on a park bench in the grounds, overlooking Lough Mahon. Far away in the harbour a small boat made its way like a slow insect; it seemed from this perspective to be set to cross the path of a dredger. Around us the air was still warm in September. He watched the boats intently now and then, and I sensed his discomfort. He had strong hands and didn't seem sure what to do with them. Beside me, she was clarity itself: clear eyes, explicit ideas, decisive gestures. My presence made them seem like complete strangers to each other, and yet they had come to me in order to understand each other.

How can anyone find God unless he or she is searching for God? I ask. And even then, is there not right and wrong searching? God cannot be part of any campaign or programme, for God is whole and not part. Her friend seemed a little more with us now and was watching me apprehensively. It was clear he had been brought here to have his arguments quelled. I feel again the painful ambiguity of talking about God. All our preoccupations bear dimly on God and yet God cannot be measured by any of them. God is wild, not domesticated. How is God to be known in this bright girl's domestication and in her friend's lack of it?

I feel the weight of their different expectations as a tension in the shoulders. At my suggestion of a walk he is the first on his feet. It is one solution to a too painful presence of another. In walking there is a rhythmic outlet for nervous energy, and a decent reason for not looking the other in the face. Besides, you can always round on the other, or be rounded on, at a key moment.

With movement he gets his courage. He was in disrepute at an early age for errors that most of humankind get away with. Since then he saw himself as an outsider and had developed the knack of inviting trouble. He had stopped practising his religion as early as he could and had a low opinion of hypocritical religious people. I wondered aloud how the tidy being beside me had set her sights on such an untidy package. Salvation, I try to say, is through the opposite, and there is a need to have the opposite, or dead, parts of the self brought to life. Through the other we may receive the courage to awaken the opposite in ourselves. There is a special providence of God in it and we are angels – messengers of God to one another. I long to be more practical for their sake, but at the same time I know that inner adjustments are a subtle matter that no one else can bring about for them.

W E HAD reached the tall gates of the Mews. This is a home within a home for my spirit. It is a cloister-like square of stone buildings from 1824. The pottery is here and the Meditation Centre with its cupola, and the ivy-covered Hermitage. Since my return from Prinknash, I have made the gift of almost all my spare time to these old buildings, coaxing them by slow steps from dereliction. And they have been transformed into a holy place by the many people who have prayed here and searched for God. It was more by instinct than design that I brought my two young friends here.

I have a strong sense of place. Our spirits are embodied in this flesh, but this flesh in turn embodies itself in the place where we are. It is a mistake to think that our being terminates at the skin. We fill a room or a house. In fact a house is an archetypal symbol of the self. For this reason, when people sit together in a room they are in a special sense – for better or worse – within each others' selves. We are not simply separate entities but interpenetrating worlds.

We climb the stairs to the meditation room. This is a place for the expansion of the spirit, for prayer, for the eternal craft of seeking God. They become silent, as even children do when they climb up here. The absence of all clutter causes a kind of hush: there is nothing to correlate to one's distractions. The bare stonework of the walls is yet warm, and the brown rafters friendly and protective. It is a single space, undivided by furniture, its focus at the far end, an icon of the Lord with a single candle before it. They pace around reverentially and he peers through each window in turn. When I suggest that we sit for a while she arranges three cushions with housewifely efficiency. Silence is comfortable here, more natural than speech.

I breathe out my spirit to the silent God. It is a kind of ritual; with the first breath I am there. God is where words muffle into nothing, more real than words, more intimate than silence. When we speak again I am aware of the transforming power of conscious silence: she is softer now and her friend is fully with us. He has a hundred questions: about the Mews, the work, the walls, the people, the pottery; and what is meditation? This last question always floors me, and I talk feebly and far too much about the search for union with God and the difficulty of this search in our time. Finally (grateful for the concreteness) I mention "The Potter" retreat-days, when people work in a meditative way with clay in the workshop below and practise sitting-meditation in this room. They will be here for sure at the next one, they assure me, and I see conviction in his face.

A T THIS stage they would like to do the 'mile-walk' in the grounds and they will return in half an hour. When they leave I enter the pottery and sit at the wheel. This is always a homecoming. The ritual of centring now works also in reverse, as all rituals do, and centring the clay is a way of centring the self. I make several unplanned pots. These are often the best, because our plans are usually the worst or deadest part of us. Nothing fails like the success of one's plans. When the self-congratulation is over there is always something dismal about it. It is like sending a Christmas-box to oneself: there is no thrill of surprise, no room for the gratuitous; it is all work and no grace.

The clay walls climb up under gentle pressure. One 'throws' a pot. This does not refer to the way that some potters unwisely slam a lump of clay onto the wheel-head before centring. (Think what this does to the bearings!) The verb 'throw' used to mean 'turn,' and this meaning has survived only in pottery. To throw a pot is to form it by this unique method of rapid turning on a wheel. It is different from all other kinds of making. Ask people to saw a piece of wood, and even if they have never done it before, they know from slicing bread how it is done. But nothing prepares one for throwing, and it is this that makes it difficult. Other kinds of making are by addition or subtraction of material; here the amount is the same from beginning to end, and the making is a reshaping.

Here at the wheel is my best place for thinking. I am a little afraid of the thinking that is done at desks; it is all too likely to be spinning out of itself. The mind can detach itself with ease from the other faculties and senses, and produce a cloth that is beautiful but unwearable.

> God guard me from those thoughts men think
> In the mind alone;
> He that sings a lasting song
> Thinks in a marrow-bone.
>> W. B. Yeats

The ironical thing about these thoughts we "think in the mind alone" is that they lay the heaviest claims to everlastingness but in fact they decompose much faster than the others. In living experience the universal is discerned by attention to the particular, and abstraction is distraction. The whole mind and body have to work in harmony at the wheel. Sometimes there are special moments when that harmony gives such a felt sense of balance and buoyancy that everything is full of light, and everything is in its own place. I have learnt to value these moments and not to judge them by less perfect ones.

A pot is made in a few minutes. Whoever invented this method six thousand years ago (or so) was a kindred spirit to Copernicus and Galileo. The potter no longer moves around the pot. Like the sun he or she stays in one place and the pot moves. *Eppur' si muove!* It was a benign technology since it did not replace the potter but demanded a new skill. The speed of throwing gives the moment a magical air. A moment ago there was nothing and now there is a kind of presence.

'Presence' is not too strong a word, for a pot is not unlike a person. It encloses a little darkness, a small mystery; it has a real interior. The irreconcilable difference between interiors and exteriors has puzzled and drawn me since childhood. Once when our home was being reconstructed, a door was opened to the outside through a wall that seemed the most reliably solid wall in the world. Places that were twenty yards apart were now together. I remember a vague feeling of outrage. The exterior had invaded the interior; and the house, the symbol of security, had been disembowelled like a rabbit. Pots too, like houses, are symbols of the self and have an inviolable secrecy. This metaphor is strengthened by the anthropomorphic language that potters use for different parts of a pot: the foot, the belly, the shoulder, the neck, the lip. And the most satisfying shapes have a discernible relation to the human body. From long looking at many pots, I know when I like a particular one: it is when my hands get itchy to pick it up, like a baby. It was with delight and recognition that I read what Kawai, a great Japanese potter, said when asked how people were to recognise good pottery. "With their bodies!" he said.

My young friends return after their walk and make enthusiastic comments about the new pots. I have to make several other shapes on request: open shapes, tall shapes, bulbous shapes…. I expound the equation between pots and people, and they make fun of identifying each other. Her spirit is like an open shape, a bowl, an uncomplicated manifestation. His is an enclosing shape, a concealment. And I recall Kierkegaard's line that depth in one's life is "a vital relationship between concealment and manifestation." If you can hear us, Søren, help these two to understand each other!

Together we inspect the new-born pots, and because of the equation we are aware that this is about something more than pots. A few have a certain meanness about them and we agree to return them to the anonymity of the lump. There are many reasons why a pot fails, but the most frequent one is when there is no energy or spirit in the way it rises from foot to lip. Then it is better not to keep it; scrape it off the wheel, with apologies, and return it to the lump. Later its clay will get another chance to come to something. If a pot has no energy in it, it is an expression of weakness and will languish in someone's cupboard, bringing no joy. The egocentric urge to think too well of one's own products has to be chastened, but without self-disgust. There has to be attachment with detachment – a difficult blend in pottery as in the rest of life. Attachment with no detachment is self-indulgent, self-enclosed; detachment with no attachment is cold, heartless, drawing its energy perhaps from self-hatred. This eye (this detached attachment) with which to look at one's pots, indeed at one's whole life, is the eye of meditation. Perhaps non-attachment is a better word. It is pure awareness. In meditation one looks with compassion at everything that arises within the self. To hate something in the self is to drive it into deeper darkness, and to indulge something in the self is to be trapped in its particular limitation. It is a great help when we can make tangible this kind of looking, when we find some *praxis,* such as pottery, through which it can stare us in the face.

They are both clearly aware that this looking at pots is also a looking at the self. It may seem an unusual way of looking, but it matters a great deal *how* one looks at the self. Some therapies, despite their bland appearance, are really a kind of aggressive tampering that cannot be good. They contain too many generalised assumptions about human beings. One such theory or generalised assumption concerns human expression in its widest sense. It is the belief that *expression* is the universal remedy. What is the solution to my anger, my fear, my hatred? "Express them!" What do I do with my loneliness? "Cough it up!" What is the meaning of my life? "Do something, do what you want." To express means 'to squeeze out'. When this becomes a general prescription it is a sort of hydraulic principle: it is about pressure and the release of pressure. Such therapies arose after the failure of the adjustment theory: "I am well because I am adjusted to society."

When society itself is seen to be unwell the individual must somehow 'produce' well-being from within him or herself, with no guidelines from without. There is nothing but one's own expression; it is a 'doing' without context. It may indeed be important to express emotions that have never been adequately expressed, but there are times when the expression of an emotion is only another way of running away from it – another way of not looking. If expression by itself were the cure, then angry people, for instance, would become less angry the more they expressed their anger. But I have seen people in therapy for years who sound more and more like a record on which the needle is slipping. Expression of an emotion is no substitute for awareness; what is needed is *expression of awareness* of an emotion. This awareness, when it is without hatred or indulgence, allows real healing to take place.

We have been talking about these things, and I feel deeply in sympathy with this young man's inexpressiveness. Somehow he is carrying his burden with dignity. If expression were thought to be his cure, then *repression* would be his disease. And there is almost nothing that cannot be seen today as repression. Suddenly one's ordinary father or mother becomes the Satan of a new religion. All structures are angrily put aside. Where, in this picture, is one's interiority? On the face of it, everything should be interiority now; but in fact there is none. There is no privacy, no inwardness, no reticence, nothing inviolable, nothing undisclosed. The self has been gutted like a rabbit. Oh, for one or two little repressions!

They have gone home now, and I am left with the ghost of Kierkegaard. I wonder what fierce truths he would shout at us if he were writing *The Present Age* today. What would he say about character, interiority, silence? To his contemporaries he said: "Superficiality is the result of doing away with the vital distinction between concealment and manifestation; it is the manifestation of emptiness."

− 3 −

Names and Things

It is not thou that shapest God;
it is God that shapeth thee.
For then thou art the work of God,
waiting the hand of the artist
who does all things in due season.
Offer God thy heart, soft and tractable,
and keep the form in which the artist has shapen thee.
Let thy clay be moist,
lest thou grow hard
and lose the imprint of God's fingers.
    St Irenaeus

The unknown has a powerful appeal, even stronger than our bondage to the familiar. Nothing would ever happen by human initiative if we were insensitive to its pull. Too much familiarity can have a deadening effect, and the greatest gifts come from beyond our small horizon.

I have to comfort myself with these thoughts as I await the arrival of twelve strangers on this Saturday morning. They are the unknown in flesh and blood. This is one of 'The Potter' retreat days, an experiment in clay and meditation. There is always this moment of recoil – a kind of hush – when I have finished being busy with preparation and can only wait. I am sitting in the meditation room and trying to be fully present. There has to be a crystallisation in the present moment after one has been too busy. I have found that the only way to be in the present moment is to be in the present *place*. Time is a fluid element, impossible to touch. The more closely we peer at it, the more microscopically it divides itself into past and future. These are not real, we assert; but where then is the reality? "I know what time is," St Augustine said, "if you do not ask me." Place, however, is entirely tangible; it is these stone walls, these rafters, this matting on the floor. I meet this place as a friend and turn back to the Lord who fills and overflows all places. I know that the only way to meet the unknown future is to be awake to the present moment, and this is done by being awake to the place one is in.

By twos and threes they arrive and make themselves known to one another, and there are awkward moments when they just stand around and look. My two young friends of last week are here and move with a kind of proprietorial air, being familiar with the place. I have learned to accept that Cork time is a little different from Greenwich time, and when everyone has arrived we climb up to the meditation room and sit in a circle on the floor. There is a multitude of cushions and meditation-stools. Unlike chairs, these small objects are not regarded as having places of their own, and so they rightly become secondary to people. Usually people sit as the furniture dictates, but when they make their own space, as now, there is almost immediately a sense of partnership.

First we have to talk freely to one another, because a silence that is created by inhibition is not silence; it is a lid held down while the pressure of steam builds up within. I try to get away with explaining as little as possible about the day. Explanations are usually a waste of time; they are an attempt to disarm the future of its challenge, to spoil its freshness: to know it before it happens and thus turn it into the past without having lived through it. If explanations could convey realities there would be no need to live. It is better to let the future be the future, to let the unknown be the unknown, until they are met face to face.

The moment of ease comes spontaneously. Now we sit in conscious silence for a few minutes. Any trace of unease that remains here is carried into the rest of the day. I need to shake off the weight of their expecta-tions – and even more, my own. I must be open to what God sends, open to Providence, which is another name for God. Providence means God in working clothes: not the God we conjure up in our minds, God working through events. I have to be explicitly aware that if anyone's life is helped by this day it will be through God's gift and not through any meddling of mine.

NOW WE are downstairs in the workshop, aproned, waiting. It is a little like one's first day at school. The simplicity of clay can be a little embarrassing, and there is a surprising vagueness about what it is. We live surrounded by objects made of clay: cups and saucers, wash-hand basins, tiles, brick houses; yet I have heard it called soil, Plasticine, plaster, putty. I give a hand-sized lump to each person, and instantly their differences from one another are visible. Some sit looking at it with curiosity but not touching it. Some glance at it and then look at me, as if to say, "What's the trick?" Some grasp it greedily and begin to maul it mercilessly. Some caress it as if it were already a Leach masterpiece.

Whoever is tempted to generalise about the present age being materialistic should stand here and watch. Most people hate or fear or are bored by matter. Clay is just straightforward matter; having no shape or size of its own, no one consistency and mainly borrowed colour, it could be said to be almost the essence of matter. It is a good indicator of one's basic attitude.

It is important not to allow oneself to be hurried along because of the impatience visible in one or two. They have to face their impatience, but it will remain invisible to them if I am carried along in its swell. This I have found to be the hardest and most selfless discipline, and it has its parallels everywhere. It is hard to be a wall against which people bounce their emotions – a wall with some 'give', of course, and one that can be injured, but nevertheless a wall. So I wait, and resist the temptation to explain.

I always work with the group, never standing apart. But as a member of the group I cannot help being aware of what is happening. I feel free to express this verbally and to make suggestions from time to time. I suggest now that they squeeze the lump of clay and look at the perfection of the palm-print on it. It is a sensitive substance, mirror-like, registering every touch of the fingers. It is much more sensitive than wood, for example, which registers only strong action with metal tools. The changing shape of the clay mirrors everything that is in the mind: haste, confusion, boredom. But I never offer interpretations of what I see. What matters is that the individual should do his or her own seeing. Others can no more do your seeing for you than they can do your eating. And anyhow this world is far too full of interpretations.

My friend of last week looks unhappy; predictably she is struggling with the dirtiness of the clay. But clay is clean dirt; it is not greasy and it washes off without soap. Dirt is said to be matter in the wrong place, but surely this is the right place. A dislike of untidiness can turn into a dislike of the earth itself. The way she is handling the clay reminds me of someone walking tip-toed on muddy ground. I sit beside her and tell her about a woman I know who never lets her children play outside in case they might dirty their clothes. "Crazy," she agrees; and then as I wait, her eyes enlarge a little with recognition. Her friend beside her rises to the occasion and smudges her forearms and face with clay. Clay makes people playful. These are moments of grace.

A lump of clay in the hand is a minor planet. It is the very stuff that planets are made of. It is feldspar rock that has disintegrated through millions of winters and summers, before there were human beings to shiver or sweat. The earliest earthenware clays began to be deposited three hundred million years ago. Some clays, called secondary clays, were washed downstream into the beds of rivers, lakes and seas. But since the surface of the earth (if the process were speeded up) is as active as the surface of a pot of boiling water, this clay can be found not only in low-lying places, but anywhere – not everywhere but anywhere. Builders and farmers hate it because it holds water and nothing grows in it. It is a headache for everyone except potters.

Now as we hold these lumps of clay I suggest an experiment. Break the lump into two lumps of equal size and make them round. Pinch from one and add to the other until they seem to be the same size and weight. Now hold one in each hand and try to discern which is heavier. (It is extremely unlikely that they have the same weight, if it came to ounces and grams.) These tiny planets, like all planets, are subject to the law of gravity. It is this force that pulls them towards the centre of the earth. I never ask for silence, for the clay does that. In their concentration they fall silent, and many tend by instinct to close their eyes. It is a wholly simplified situation: the body alone is being asked a question; the mind has nothing to offer. Perhaps the closing of the eyes and the mouths signifies this; and, as if to confirm it, I notice that many by instinct lift their forearms from the table. The body is saying, "Let the message through."

It is a pleasure to watch people becoming sensitive in their bodies. These friends are rapt in effortless concentration, and there is softness in their faces such as people have when they pray. What a transparent miracle the body is! But how we exploit and dishonour it! The apparent cult of the body in these times is not one thing; it is many things together, good and bad, with only the *word* 'body' in common. There is a new sensitivity about diet, fitness, rhythms.... But there is also the world of fashion and cosmetics, which is a multi-million dollar industry, and its advertising method is a cult of *image,* not body. Unlike any actual body this is quite abstract, and many people think badly of themselves for not having a body that matches the current image. This contempt for one's actual body is the fatal weakness that makes people fair game for the advertising industry. There is a special pathos about heavy make-up; however glamorous the effect, there is a cringing person behind it. But when I look now at my friend with clay on her face, I am reassured that here in the Mews, 'body' means actual body and not 'image'.

This absurdly simple weighing of two lumps of clay in the hands is an exercise in being-in-the-body, Faced with this task we would normally reach for a kitchen scales; in other words, we would bypass the sensitivity of the body and let a gadget be sensitive in our stead. We fill our lives with gadgets, every one of which helps us to be less sensitive. We alienate our sensitivity, becoming more and more empty and dead. An alive person cannot be exploited, only a half-dead one. Anyone who comes along can exploit people who, for example, feel hungry when the clock tells them to be hungry. The body itself has an exquisite sense of timing, but if we never allow ourselves to depend on it, it grows duller and duller till we hardly know day from night.

I stand watching this easy concentration in people's faces as they hold the lumps of clay still, or roll them back and forth in their hands, or sometimes change them from hand to hand. There is good sense in this, for the hand we use most is stronger and therefore the clay will seem lighter in it. I have told them to try to sense, as if their lives depended on it, which lump is heavier. They hardly look like people whose lives are at stake, but that is better; real concentration is effortless. The strain we associate with concentration is because of lack of concentration; when concentration is full there is no strain.

I try to read from them, rather than from my watch, the right moment to move on. "Make something – anything!" This is the signal for a thousand inhibitions to arise together. We are taught to be owners and users of things, but not creators. This teaching begins early: nowhere is it so clearly seen than in the world of children's toys. Everything is perfect, finished: the toy car has a motor in it and moves by itself; the dolly wets her diaper. Nothing is left to the imagination. The child is being asked to relate to the toy only as an owner and user, not as a creator. We are training them already to be perfect little capitalists and fair game for the advertisers.

"I can't make anything," one man says, having scarcely tried. It catches on: "I'm no good at this kind of thing," says someone else. This critic in us is the enemy within. How can we live all day with a critic who criticises even *before* one has done anything? There has to be the compassionate eye that looks with neither rejection nor indulgence: this is right criticism. But the other critic is a neurotic tyrant, drawing his energy from fear and self-contempt, never wanting anything to happen, good or bad.

After gentle coaxing (but some need no coaxing at all) they are on their way. Very quickly the tables are covered with bowls, dishes and mugs with large handles; swans are popular, probably because clay is good for making the curved neck; there are a few human forms, and some shapes that seem to have come straight from the Land of Id; and there is always someone making something like an apple-tart! (We all start from the familiar, do we not?)

Soon there are several who have that look of being finished but not satisfied. I have talked a little to them about the critic who only wants to stand by the wall and criticise, so it is important now to leave them to face this critic who has robbed them of their power. "Who is drilling his or her eyes through the back of your neck?" I ask. Your critic is certainly you, but a part of you that has grown in symbiosis with some outside critic: a parent, an older brother or just other people. You must look at your work with your own eyes, with the eye of compassion, and become free in it.

As soon as people become a little free in their work there arises, in a lively group, a great wave of humour that has a beautiful quality. Laughter can be many things: nervous, sarcastic, taunting, crude, demented, cynical. It can be a technique for getting by without facing oneself or others, or a cover for hostility, or a systematic method of ridiculing others in order to magnify oneself and strengthen one's prejudices.... But here, it seems to be uncomplicated; it is a laughter that springs from a compassionate awareness of our own contradictions. We would love to soar, but we have big feet; we could be free but we bind ourselves in chains; we want to possess creativity but we become possessed by what we create. This kind of laughter springs from a compassionate awareness that we are, in the poet's words, "the glory, jest and riddle of the world." Who knows the meaning of this humour, or wants to know? There is a kind of knowing that destroys its object. All I know is that one touches that same underground vein of humour quite often in meditation. It is a relief to find that the spiritual life is the funniest of all adventures.

The finished product can be a powerful enemy. We can be making a mug or a jug, but in human reality it may be a ball and chain. We become trapped by the *idea* of the product and we either rush towards it in self-forgetfulness, disrespecting the materials, or else we become mesmerised and unable to move at all. As a way out of this impasse I

suggest we make *something that has no name*. It is the finished product
that is given a name, so in detaching names we have become free of all
productivity-thinking. This freedom works magic. Now it is possible
to enjoy the journey and not fret about the destination as we always do,
pawning the present for a future that will never redeem it.

Within ten minutes there is an extravagant array of shapes before
us. What a welcome rest from mass-production! Almost every product
around us today is standardised – in other words it is an exact replica of
its *idea*. If it is different in any way from its idea, and therefore from the
others of its kind, it becomes a "second," a reject. This standardisation is
necessary for mass-production, but the cost is a great visual impoverish-
ment of the world and a dulling of one's appreciation of difference. Our
minds drift into the groove of simply comparing things: nothing is seen
for itself but only as it is like or unlike something else. Slowly we come
to live in a more and more boring world. But one who sees something for
itself will not think of comparing it. So, for the space of an hour, away
with names, away with ideas of things, away with standard products! Fill
the world – or just for the moment this workshop! – with creatures of
your own fantasy, shapes that startle you as they come into being under
your hands, inventions in the literal sense: things *found,* not planned in
your head or on a drawing-board. "I don't create," said Picasso, "I invent."

Picasso would probably not feel out of place among these amazing
shapes that arise and disappear in a continual flow. One effect of detaching names is that you never know when the job is finished. This means
that one shape flows into the next by degrees that are themselves shapes.
It is a process.

This detachment from names and the corresponding awareness
of process is an important part of meditation. God is free of our poor
shackles; God is "above names" as Meister Eckhart put it. Here too, the
names we put on God are like 'finished products' of thinking. What? Do
I mean that we should brush aside *all words* – meaning all Scriptures, all
Liturgies, all the writings of the saints and mystics? No – no more than
we should smash all Sung vases or hack down every work of ceramic

art. There have been people who knew God and whose words, consequently, are not shabby mass-productions but pure light. To make a space within where these words can be heard, we need to brush aside a great deal of mass-production, for our thoughts are often carbon-copies and our lives a mimicry. The Meister, who was himself one of the greatest of the mystics, said:

> We can find no name that we could give to God, but we are permitted the names the saints called him by, whose hearts were regenerated by God and flooded with light.

And it is precisely when we try to fashion in our own hearts an honest home-made prayer that the sacred writings open to us – just as we come to appreciate great pottery when we begin to make some humble pots ourselves. Yes, but do these sacred words then somehow 'contain' God for us? The only word that can contain God is God's own Word, the Word made flesh, "the Way." Other words are pointers to the Way. A way is a process, a movement. What counts is that our spirit should move along the way to God and not halt at words and names, "for God is above names and ineffable."

Now that it is near lunch-time, I ask them if they have really learnt detachment from finished products, from ideas of things, from names; and whether they are happy to be for the time being in movement, in process. "Oh yes," in unison. "Then," I say, "you won't find it difficult to return what you have made to the lump from which it came!" The idea of detachment is beautiful but the actual moment of detachment looks like a loss, a small death.

All the small acts of detachments are rehearsals for the big one. When the big one comes it will take our breath away, and we shall meet the unknown face to face.

Words and Silence

If one knows anything of God and affixes any name to it, that is
not God. A good man was praying to God and wanted to give
God names. Then a brother said, 'Be silent, you dishonour God.'
  Meister Eckhart

Stone, like clay, is a friendly natural substance. These two are one in fact:
clay is just stone in semi-liquid form. Stone bears the history of the planet
in itself, and it is nearly always local history – few enjoy transporting
stone over long distances. Its shapes and sizes convey a refreshing sense
of the fortuitous, and its colours are easy on the eye.

As we sit in silence in the meditation room, waiting for the last to
arrive, these stone walls are speaking to us in their very silence and
humility. They are honest, having no covering of plaster or paint. And
they speak of the humble lives of the long-forgotten men who put them
there with skill. Meditation is many things, but it is always about essential
honesty, the unmasking of one's own false pretences, the discovery of
the compassionate heart.

Most people have no preconceptions about clay. This is what makes
it a delight to work with: there is a sense of starting from the beginning,
and this always gives a beautiful freshness and openness to the mind.
These are the qualities that enable us to do more essential learning in
our first five years than we do for the rest of our lives. But our minds
become old and obtuse and clogged with preconceptions. When it comes
to meditation these qualities of freshness and openness may well be
missing. The mind is all too likely to be filled with knowledge that has
not been bought at the full price of experience. It is therefore necessary

to speak to one another about meditation – not in order to say what it is (how can you say what the taste of a lemon is?) but in order to let the mind play out its distractions.

Is it the same as prayer? Is it different from contemplation? Is it an Eastern thing? Does it mean relaxation? Do you make your mind a blank? What do you get out of it?

In an age of ecumenism the temptation is to think that every truth must be a global truth from beginning to end. By 'global', in this context, people often mean Indian or Japanese or Tibetan. No doubt the world's great religions are nearer to one another in their deepest reaches than they are at the surface. But we must not make a false claim to be already in the deepest reaches. Those who are make no such claims, and they have reached there by being truthfully who they are and not by pretending to be someone else. We are not Indians, we are from the Western world. The truth of our faith must manifest itself to us in our own house. In 1946 Alan Watts wrote that "the Church has in its possession, under lock and key (or maybe the sheer weight of persons sitting on the lid), the purest gold of mystical religion."

My own path has been a roundabout one, and it makes me remember the story of Chesterton who set out from his London home one day with large suitcases. When a friend asked where he was going, he said: "To London – via New York, California, Tokyo, Athens." Sometimes we see our own place best from a distance. For more than ten years I have had a lively interest in Eastern religions and I am much taken by Zen in particular. It seems to have a quality that resonates with my spirit better than anything else I have found. Then, through a friend whom I met in Zen circles, I discovered the Rhineland mystics – in particular Meister Eckhart, Tauler and Suso. In these I found everything I had been looking for in Zen – and more. The irony of it took a while to sink in: these were not only Westerners, Europeans, Christians, but they were all Dominicans! It was by this indirect route that I had come upon treasures that had lain in the libraries of every community I had lived in for twenty years. I had gone around the world to discover my own house.

It has taught me an appreciation of the immediate.

Must we thirteen people speak to one another of past and present, East and West, as we sit together in this concrete place at this particular time? It would only be a wandering away from ourselves. Instead let the question be: what is each one here seeking at this moment? Perhaps I am not consciously seeking God at all. This may be the deepest *implication* of my search, but if it is not my conscious search at this moment, let me not pretend that it is. If I am not consciously seeking God but only a relaxation technique, then meditation is just that for me at this moment. When I am tired of relaxing I may then want something else, such as the ability to cope with my anger or depression. Then let meditation be a relentless gazing at my anger or my depression until I can see its shape. I cannot normally see the shape of my emotions, being in them as in a fog. The kind of looking that is meditation is a search for the truth of my emotions; it is more than a way of controlling them. Thus it has a way of always inviting me beyond my ego-centred plans for my own betterment. I will inevitably spend some time – perhaps half a lifetime – in the double-bind of spiritual self-improvement. When this falls away from me, through insight, I may be found by the real God and I may get the courage not to run and hide my nakedness with theories, projects and foolish arguments.

We have been experimenting with posture, and there is an occasional bustle as someone abandons a meditation-stool for the luxury of a cushion, or ventures the semi-lotus. Whatever seating one uses, the essential is that the spine should retain its natural curves, so that the body is balanced. It is a matter of finding the most easeful posture. We can cheat ourselves here, for we are used to enduring soft armchairs that only have the appearance of comfort. Posture is important: the way we hold and carry the body is the way we hold and carry our spirit, for the body is the visible shape of the spirit. The idea of relaxation as 'flop down' is a disowning of the body and therefore of the whole self. There can be no sense of one's own presence when the body is simply dumped in some convenient space.

I notice that my friend is sitting with great self-possession. There is no greater joy in the world than to see someone come home who has experienced his life as a banishment. It must be God already at work, pulling in our orbit after the banishment from Eden. I have to resist a strong temptation to praise this strong posture, for that would make him self-conscious and therefore divided once again from himself.

A candle burns before the icon. This is a fifteenth-century Byzantine image of the Lord. The hands draw one's attention to the heart; the face is dark and strong. It is an image of the Sacred Heart, in a sense, but this is visible only in the gesture; the heart remains within. It is in strong contrast with the images of repository art. These show a wounded heart that has been displaced from within the body. This is a caricature of interiority; it is the inner world turned out, like a pocket. Such a heart, like such a pocket, could hold nothing at all. "Through a chink too wide there comes in no wonder." The icon, in contrast, does not beg your pity or whine about your sins. It shows the strong Lord of the Gospels revealing the inner world in which God's Kingdom must strike root.

In modern languages the heart is associated with the emotion of love. But in the Scriptures it was not associated with any emotion in particular; it was rather a symbol of the whole inner life of a person. Great damage has been done to religious sensibility by forcing and feigning the emotion of love. It has put simulation where there should be a relentless truthfulness.

In reply to a question about the difference between meditation and contemplation a stock-still man at the side says he has gone into this. In older language, he explains, 'meditation' used to mean prayerful reflection or points to ponder, while 'contemplation' meant a silent presence to God. And there was an important distinction between the kind of silent contemplation one managed to enter by one's own efforts, and the kind that was from beyond – a gift. However, in modern language, the wide world uses the word 'meditation' to refer to silent presence, whether to God or oneself or something else; and for the most part Christians have gone along with this change of words, so that when they now talk about meditation they often mean the activity they used to call 'contemplation'.

Someone picks up the word 'activity' and asks, "What does one *do?*" To say "nothing" is not much help, because it gives the impression that the mind has to become a blank. This is one of the chief caricatures of meditation, and it is very unhelpful, for it sends one off in the wrong direction. Meditation is about being more awake and alert than usual, not less so. It is about using all of one's intelligence – which means perception, not learning. It means being alive in all one's being: body, mind and spirit. There is a current vogue for disparaging the mind. It is easy to see what is meant, for the mind's style is often baroque, unable to allow even the smallest empty space. But it would be wrong to reject it just because it often works badly. Meditation is not a way of subtracting a dimension from ordinary life but of realising a deeper one. The mind should not be rejected but distilled to its essence, which is intelligence, or more particularly, the act of perception. From working at the potter's wheel I have seen that the privileged moment for seeing all the faculties in harmony, and the part each one plays, is *when I am doing something right* and not when I am philosophising about the mind. So, to the question, "what does one do?" I can only reply that one should first do some work (with clay or washing dishes or digging in the garden), making sure to move with sensitivity and awareness; and then sit still in the presence of God without letting these qualities fade.

"But should I talk to the Father or Jesus or ask the Holy Spirit to come to me?" There I have no 'should' to offer you, for your spirit is an inviolable place, and the Father calls you by name, not by batch. If words begin to bubble to the surface from some deep place, what pre-cast principle could tell you to reject them? And if you have not let your sensitivity and awareness fade, you will not be tempted to fill every empty space with words in case God should come too near. A ban on words would be as arbitrary as a ban on silence. St Teresa of Avila wrote: "Do not be attached to any form of words … nor to silence either."

The conversation has burnt itself out and we make ready for meditation. It is a great delight to see twelve crystallised presences. Mental alertness and the absence of it are always visible in the body. We have all spent so many years in the captivity of the classroom that we expect every group of people sitting together in this formation to be only reluctantly awake.

I ring a small bell at the beginning and at the end, for clarity's sake, to avoid woolly edges. There is no need at present to talk about breathing, for if posture is right the breathing will not be wrong. It is enough to recommend loosening tight belts, for these prevent abdominal breathing.

With the sound of the bell silence falls and the meditation room seems to sing. They are totally different, the silence of an empty room and the silence of a room full of silent people. Presence alone has great power and we usually undervalue it. This is the subtle thing we bring to God: our presence. If we think or talk as well, it is not for God's sake but our own.

The time passes quickly, but sometimes when I ring the bell at the end of twenty minutes or thirty minutes, a few people have come to look like wilted flowers, and it is mysterious to wonder where the bright presences are now. No doubt the Lord takes care of us just as well when we are asleep, but in his time he did go around saying – perhaps shouting – "wake up!" In Zen there is a highly effective method of keeping meditators awake: when people lose their alertness – and Zen masters have hawks' eyes for this – they get a whack of a stick called *kyosaku*, the 'awakening stick': not out of anger or impatience but out of compassion. It is a work of compassion to wake up a drowsy soul!

Such a method may seem a little rugged to us, but in fact the kind of probing into others' souls that some schools of spirituality practise is much more violent. As in some therapies, this kind of probing is violent even to the point of telling you that you must not defend yourself – while yet it uses the language of gentleness. I don't have much stomach for this, and I am glad that the Order in which I have grown from late teens has never put an emphasis on having one's own spiritual director. The wisdom and life of the Order itself is one's spiritual guide. The individual conscience has an inviolable inwardness through which all real vitality comes, and it is led to God by being in a graced community rather than by being interfered with by someone equally in need of wisdom. Many people go from one therapy weekend to another, not to solve their problems but in a forlorn search for intimacy. I am sometimes much afraid that the same dynamic may be operating on a wider but less visible scale in the spiritual life. Our inner life, which is our most shining gift, can also become our greatest burden. When we have little strength in ourselves and the burden seems difficult to bear, we may certainly find strength from another person – one who accompanies us for a few paces or a few miles along the spiritual path. But such a one is a companion, not a director.

We can do much violence to ourselves and others at this deep level of meditation. Any attempt to coerce our spirit into attitudes and emotions that it is not ready for, is violence. Or when we try to prolong or repeat some spiritual experience we have had, we are dealing violently with our spirit. All such violence breeds a reaction in our deepest places, and I have met many who have come to hate God and themselves – though, with the same violence, they prevent that thought from shaping itself. This need to interfere with every living thing is a modern disorder, and it becomes rampant in the absence of a contemplative outlook. It is fundamentally a hatred of life, for who would want to mince up the human spirit unless he or she privately hated it? A wound may indeed need to be cleaned – though, left to itself, the body is able to do this by bleeding – and it is then left to heal from within. Likewise what a wounded mind or spirit needs is not continual intrusion but a place or community that surrounds it with compassion.

WE HAVE been sitting together and talking about these things. It is a conversation that retains the atmosphere of meditation: it is very easy, and most feel no need to fill in every crevice of silence with words. But a few want to reveal everything that took place in them during the meditation session. The syntactical indecision of what they say is worth noticing. Sometimes it begins as a question and tails off into a sharing; sometimes it is the other way around; and sometimes it sits in the air not knowing how to land, nor even why it is flying at all. Times without number I have been deeply moved by the way a group has helped such a person. The help has not occurred by taking up the details of what was said, but by the quality of their presence. It is precisely this quality of sympathetic presence and silence that enables us to hear our own words. I was blessed years ago in a confrere who showed me this.

Now a question arises that I had sidestepped at the beginning: "What does one get out of meditation?" I am doubly glad that I was not pressed on this before the session. Firstly, I would have felt like a politician making promises; and even if I had promised nothing I would still have sounded like one, for they sometimes make a great show out of promising nothing. Secondly, I can now let the group shape a reply to the question. "Peace, relaxation;" "a sense of God's presence;" "my problems seemed very far away." But is this *why* one meditates? Is it to gain these feelings and sensations? "No," says my friend, "because drugs could do that for you," and perhaps he spoke from experience. Then why? "It could be a sort of anchor in life." But if you meditated every day for a week and never once in that time experienced it as an anchor, what would you do? "I would probably give it up." Does this not show that it is still a drug – an anchoring-drug? "I think that if someone takes up medita-tion they should stick with it even at times when it doesn't appear to be paying off," said his friend beside him; and I see what a perfect match they are, not because they are alike but because they are so different. But *why* does one stick with it, I ask her; is it in the hope of future pay-off? "No, you stick with your friend, for example, not just because he makes you laugh or takes away your loneliness, but because he is your friend, There's no 'why' to it."

They are answering their own question, so they will not have to carry the answer as a load on the mind. It is the act of their own intelligence. Only undigested thoughts have weight.

I recall that Heidegger said the attitude of modern people to nature is like their attitude to a filling station: they take what they want and drive away. We learn to exploit everything, even our own experience. So widespread and deep is this that it takes great perception, as in my two friends, to step beyond it. Everything has to serve some other end, and present experience is tolerated only because it points to something else. This is nowhere clearer than when someone keeps saying, "So what?" to everything. This attitude is really a hatred of actual existence, for we only *look* for purposes and rewards when we hate what we are doing: "I fast twice a week, I give tithes of all that I possess." He had kept a careful account. But no one would say: "I have been singing in the bath for forty years; what reward will I have?" Meditation means being fully present to God who gives you everything you are capable of receiving *in this moment,* but who never yet gave anyone the future.

Now that we have done further clearance work, we set ourselves once more to meditate. And we make a resolution that we will not talk about it when it is over. This cuts the root of a very subtle distraction: that of meditating in order to have something to say about it afterwards. This would be a crowning irony.

The sound of the little bell is clearer than all our words.

I am not searching for God because He is not hiding. His promise is "I am with you always"
when that promise comes home to roost there will be a natural falling away of the distracting encumbrances that bar the way to seeing with the 'Eye of Faith' what has been there all the while. "I will NEVER leave you or forsake you!"
Our own preoccupation with the labour of carrying the luggage of a lifetime around is what causes us to a blindness of what is otherwise abundantly clear!
God loves us, and wants to make His home in us, but the door is only able to be opened from our side! Gracious, Heavenly Father, welcome — do come in!

– 5 –

Symbol and Reality

Listen again, One evening at the Close
Of Ramazan, ere the better Moon arose,
In that old Potter's shop I stood alone
With the clay Population round in Rows.
And strange to tell, among that Earthen Lot
Some could articulate, while others not:
And suddenly one more impatient cried –
'Who is the Potter, pray, and who the Pot?'
    Omar Khayyam

Put a group of twelve people in a room together and it is probable that in an hour's time they will have splintered into several small groups, that most of them will still not know one another, and that there will be at least two of them arguing about politics.

Put a bag of clay in the room with them and the transformation is profound: they become a community and attain a degree of freedom with one another that no amount of talking could have brought about. Perhaps it takes a natural element to make us natural. Think of all the serious-minded businessmen who shout and kick ball like children when they are near the sea – a thing unimaginable on the street.

We are working again with clay. After some time I suggest we allow something to take shape that may be symbolic of one's life. I point out that it is important not to begin with an idea, for then there is no discovery. An idea is a destination, but all real discoverers set out into the unknown. In a short time there is an immense, effortless concentration, almost like that of children – and deep silence.

A new medium, such as clay, does not simply express the same things in another way. There is genuine newness, for each new medium brings another part of us to life. It happens in a moment. Something 'clicks', we say; and it is a good word, for it is the opposite of 'woolly'. The moment when someone finds his or her new medium is a precise one, like a click, however uncertain and woolly the preceding moments may have been. I wait for these visible clicks around me, and it is nearly always a surprise to the one who has it. A new vitality is visible because something in the person has risen from the dead.

At such moments I am awestruck at the power of living symbolism. I have no doubt that we live by symbols. Unlike abstract ideas they have roots that draw power from every level of the self, and so they bring these levels to life – as plants can be said, in a special sense, to bring the earth to life.

Everywhere fingers are smoothing and pinching and squeezing. Your hands are your power, your efficacy, the force of your life. God moved in the Old Testament "with a mighty hand and an outstretched arm." At the other extreme the man in the Gospel who had a withered hand had no creative power at all. Perhaps he had disowned it, for it is life that causes us the most fear, not death. And you, like everyone else, have false friends who prefer you dead – or at any rate not quite alive. They may be dead themselves and needing company. You are predictable as long as you are dead, but if you become alive no-one can be entirely sure – not even yourself – what you will do next. When the Lord healed that man's withered hand on the Sabbath, the Pharisees were furious for they were legalists and had a special interest in keeping God's power in the proper channels and keeping people predictable. He was sent to set prisoners free; and we make prisoners of ourselves with invisible manacles. I have a sad friend who has fled from the pain of life into the bleak Nirvana of alcoholism, and I have noticed his hands become less and less alive, till the fingers scarcely oppose one another any more. I sometimes draw his attention to it in the hope that such an image of death may shock him back to life.

Once, a group of gifted children were brought here by their harassed parents. I had always thought that the higher a child's intelligence, the happier a parent would be, but it seems it is not so. Exceptionally high intelligence is a little like cancer, for it devours other areas of one's life. I remember one ten-year-old whose face was red with frustration as he clawed at the clay. I sat beside him and enquired how he was getting on. "I can't *think* of anything to make," he said. When I suggested that he shouldn't bother to think about it but let his hands make something – something that was never before seen on the earth – he objected: "But hands are bad things; they are for hitting and fighting." I was amazed to see the disequilibrium of the age mirrored so perfectly in so young a person.

Then on reflection I saw that it was *because* he was so bright that he was such a perfect mirror, and if any of us had been a complete success in our education we would be just like him. A little stupidity may be a saving grace, for it allows the other gifts a space in which to grow.

Though my twelve adult friends here are full of enthusiasm, I wonder how silly most of them would feel if any of their friends from work walked through the door. There is nothing quite like mockery or incomprehension to kill a new gift or a new insight.

One very intense and angular man is making a tall shape that is having difficulty staying up, and he has to buttress it on every side. He is frowning at it, unaware that his elbows are getting in his neighbour's way as he adds another buttress. His difficulty, he explains, is that since everything is made of clay, the difference between the shape and its buttresses is not clear enough; and the whole thing together looks uncouth. "Those bits," says his neighbour, indicating the buttresses, "are like elbows." They are enjoying one another's company and this playful banter goes on. There is a belief in serious atmospheres for this kind of work, but who is to say that fun isn't better? After all, children do most of their real learning through play and fun.

There is no attempt to invade this man's privacy and to extract some interpretation; but since he is talking freely about what he has made it is right to listen. In any case the language of clay is highly symbolic and does not pin a person to the wall in the way that psychological interpretation can do.

When he looks at this ungraceful object, he says, it is clear to him that it is a startlingly accurate image of his life. He has always had a compelling urge to be a success and to get ahead of others. But he has a knack of involving others in his projects, not for their sakes but his own. Why the urge, here, to make something so tall that it has to be supported by buttresses? He has been using people as buttresses to his own ambition. He has made this shape all by himself, so it reflects inner, not outer, conditions. His wife has often told him that he creates an atmosphere of fuss and dependency wherever he goes, but this has never stared him in the face so vividly as now. This image, he is certain, will stay in his memory and haunt him every time he attempts to continue the old pattern.

A girl in woolly jumpers has very quickly made a pattern of encircling shapes and is contemplating it intently. I stress again that there is no need to talk about what one has made; it is more important to let the shape do the talking. There is no reason why its meaning should be clear straight away, and talking about it may fix it prematurely. Its meaning may not be clear for days or months, for our symbol-making ability is far ahead of our conscious minds. Nevertheless this girl has seen something and wants to talk. She is surprised at how quickly this shape has appeared and at how inevitable it seems. Because a series of totally encircling shapes would be very boring, she has varied it by allowing some parts to be outside the circles. But this is causing her an inexplicable unease, far out of proportion to everything that lies visible; so it may be symbolic.

"How would you change it if you wanted to be completely comfortable with it?" I ask. It would be just concentric circles, she says, a very boring pattern. "Are you comfortable only when you are bored?" asks the angular man, pouncing with great enthusiasm, and I gasp with apprehension.

There is nothing more vulnerable in this world than an undefended self, and I am afraid lest anyone should feel stripped-down at the end of this day. She does not take fright, however. It is clear to her that she has always been looking for protection and security: this is the meaning of the enclosing circles. Yet she always ended by despising any person who provided her with protection and security. She had ended several friendships because she was bored by them, yet she was afraid of anyone who might take her out of her depth. "You haven't met the right man yet!" says my angular friend, and I cannot feel sorry for him when she turns on him and says she does not want to be patronised, that she is not waiting around to be rescued by some hero, and that there are men who have an insufferable tendency to see themselves in that role. He looks deflated but he will live, and it was a salutary lesson. "Were you looking for security and protection just now as you were doing battle?" I ask her. No, she was not. Was she pleased that she had struck out? Yes, very happy with herself. Then, enclosing circles are not the full story. I see from them that there is no enmity. People often help one another by accident.

My young friends, working side by side, are making very frequent cross-references. It is clear that they are getting ready to give an account of themselves. Like the other girl, she has made a round shape. Not only is the shape itself round, but all the small objects within its circle are also round and perfect. There are spheres and hemispheres, rings and collars and disks, and all of these are arranged in circular patterns. It is perfect in the literal sense of the word: it is completed.

Her friend has not made one thing but several, a loose configuration of very unfinished shapes. They might have just happened and not been made at all. She wants him to talk about them but he is reluctant and disowns them by moving away. I ask him if he would like to talk about hers. He would. It reminds him of his little sister's 'cabildy house' in the garden, or a doll's house. That's all. He had said this to her a while ago, she said, and she was still thinking about it. She saw his shapes as a kind of refusal of responsibility. There was nothing definite in them, no commitment to anything. Even the way he walked away from them expressed this. It seemed natural for him to be against everything, never for anything. Someone asks if they now understand one another better, and makes the suggestion that they work *together* to make another shape.

They set to it together with such earnestness that I think of two birds building a nest, and perhaps it is not altogether different: they are creating a symbolic shared space in which to live.

"Make something funny!" I say to the others on an impulse, anxious that we are becoming too solemn.

This time they will keep the objects they have made. You can only keep what you are not attached to; if you are attached to something, the tables are turned and *it* keeps you. Very quickly, and with a lot of giggles and whoops of laughter, the tables begin to swarm with prodigious shapes. Every species on earth, it seems, could find its missing link here.

As the time goes by I notice that this merriment is dying down and people are becoming quieter. To my utter astonishment I see a woman with tears streaming down her face. I want to apologise, oh sorry, but that is absurd. Whatever underground vein she has struck is an overflowing one, but I have not bulldozed her into anything.

What makes us so afraid of tears, as if they were a bad thing? Is it that we are afraid of emotions? Or is it the uncontrolled that terrifies us? Or simply reality? Whatever evasions and qualifications we are able to build into our words, tears are unmistakably real. The angular man offers a Kleenex, a kind of sacrament. If you want to know what we can really do for one another, look now: a crumpled Kleenex to say, "I have been there too."

The rest of us are not sure what to do or say, so we bury ourselves deeper in our 'funny' objects. If she told us what was wrong we could turn it over in our minds and offer advice, but direct emotion is different from an opinion or a statement. It is the full presence of another. And why do we presume that something is *wrong?* It may be that something is right at last. It may be that this woman has been wishing for years that she could cry and it has happened now. She probably has no theories about it; she did not work herself up to a catharsis, as I have seen people do. She is just crying like a child, the tears running down her face, and she makes no attempt to dry them. Children cry a lot, and no doubt it does them good; and they do not feel embarrassed by it or try to stop one another. Perhaps the cathartic people, after all, are only swinging to the opposite extreme from society at large. There must be thousands of novels and films where the strong man, as Dorothy Sayers said, reacts to great personal loss "by a slight compression of the lips and by throwing his cigarette into the fireplace."

"I just feel a great sadness," she manages to say, no more. But why should she begin to feel sadness during the funny part? It must be that, deep down, fun and sadness are one, as different countries and continents are one beneath the sea. We know that clowns are often sad, that our own saddest moments can occur when we are in the midst of celebration. When we experience any emotion deeply we are more alive, and therefore more vulnerable to its opposite as well. Could it be that laughter and weeping are only halves and that the whole is when we laugh and weep at once? Someone who laughs in order not to weep is clinging to one side, and such laughter has no joy or healing in it; it rings hollow. At the heart of laughter there is weeping; could it be that at the heart of weeping there is laughter? There must be some meaning in the fact that they look so alike on the outside.

The man beside her put his arm around her shoulder for a moment and then went back to his clay. It was a perfect action, neither flight nor intrusion. The most fundamental process is the meeting of pain with compassion. A quiet woman says, "It is right to be able to cry and women understand it well." Men are not allowed to cry, for we still have our stereotypes. Countless men all over the world have an image of what they should be (for they were all boys once): John Wayne, astride his horse, yelling at his enemies, "the hell I will!"

Is it possible to experience joy if we try to insulate ourselves against sorrow? At funerals I have heard many faint homilies about joy that simply left everyone forlorn. It often happens that a person discovers, years later, that he or she has not sufficiently mourned the death of a parent or a friend. To grieve is to *suffer* the loss of someone you love, and to suffer means 'to allow'. To grieve, then, is to allow the pain of life and death to reach you; and it shows that you are not made of ice. If you swallow down your grief or pretend that you are not feeling it, you put on a layer of insensitivity which then becomes part of you. And so you become insensitive not only to death but to life as well. You cannot be sensitive to life while fleeing the thought of death. Death gives our life a saltiness, a poignancy, an unrepeatable quality. Without its opposite death – life would be a faded thing. Let old soldiers fade away if they want to, but I think I'd prefer to die.

She begins to talk about the clay shape that was the occasion of her sadness. It started out as a funny animal with a round belly and changed into a round-bellied pot. It became a symbol of the great emptiness she felt in her life. This was something she had always managed to avoid looking at directly and so she led an extremely busy life. But here it was staring her in the face. The directness and the pathos of this simple pot had moved her deeply and as she held it in her hands her tears had run down and fallen into it.

The compassion of the group is like a meditation: neither obtrusive attachment nor yet detachment but the better part of both. I am about to ask if she is all right now when I realise what an empty question that would be. We are children of a problem-solving age; our urge is "right, let's move on!" But where are we going? Can the pain of a brother or sister be left behind? Time moves on and we may have to leave another to solitude, but let us not leave them as if they were a problem solved or a problem put aside as we rush to the next problem. We can never 'solve' another's life; what an ego-trip that would be! We can never simply pick another person up – unless we intend to carry them as baggage for the rest of our life or till we get tired of them. We cannot help a suffering brother or sister by being strong in their stead, keeping them weak, nor by becoming weak with them. We help them by being strong and stay-ing beside them in case they need us as they struggle to their own feet.

Our young friends have finished. There was a special providence for them in the woman's tears. It meant that the atmosphere in which they worked was not one of rivalry with each other but of genuine human feeling. Each said in a different way that it had become clear as they worked that what mattered most was not fighting one's own campaign or gaining an inch for oneself, but having a heart for the other's difficulty. It became clear to them that as they set out to make their mark on the world there would always be the sound of weeping brothers and sisters.

– 6 –

Bread and Wine

No love that in a family dwells,
No carolling in frosty air,
Nor all the steeple-shaking bells
Can with this single Truth compare
That God was Man in Palestine
And lives to-day in Bread and Wine.
John Betjeman

God made the world like a huge football and kicked it out into space, and that was such a powerful kick that it is still sailing through the sky, and when it lands I suppose that will be the end of the world.

It was, at any rate, the end of my childhood religion when it was impressed on me that "you can't say that!" This overbearing judgment fell like a tree across the road, for we think of God as we can and seldom as we should. Children, especially, have their own theology and it is a wildly animated one, for as James Stephens said:

With children thought cannot be separated from action for very long. They think as much with their hands as with their heads. They have to do the thing they speak of in order to visualise the idea.

It would be a close description of the way we have been behaving during this day. As we sit here in a circle this evening in the meditation room to celebrate the Eucharist, it occurs to me that the Eucharist only unfolds itself to childlike people – who have to do the thing they speak of. I have always noticed that the Eucharist seems perfectly in place here at the end of such a day. It is in a context that is congenial to it: earthy, symbolic, meditative. It is sad to see the Eucharist sometimes reduced to words and explanations, not allowed to speak for itself in its own language.

I am aware again of the freedom from furniture and the power that this gives. Whenever I celebrate the Eucharist where there are rows of seats, I feel a nagging urge to apologise to the people who are further away. This is certainly the age of small groups if our inner hunches are right. Perhaps I read too much into the text when I pause at the point where the Lord told the people to sit down on the grass to eat the bread *in small groups* – not in a crowd and not in solitude. Occasionally when I enter a traditional church I am not insensitive to the power of the open spaces there: it is about God being greater than our hearts. But I must admit that most of these churches chill me to the bone. No doubt they were made to be full, not to be empty; but even when they are full, many of them look impersonal, almost empty. Polished marble has repelled me all my life. It may be cool and lovely for people who live too much in the sun, but it gives me a feverish shiver in an Irish church, for it is often damp as well as cold. There was an Irish tradition that hell was cold rather than hot, and I hope that whoever began the custom in Ireland of imitating Italian churches is now in a warmer place!

There are people who would find this meditation room (once a grain-loft) an incongruous place for the Eucharist; but they would probably have misgivings about the Last Supper too. I have celebrated the Eucharist in Notre Dame, in Paris, and in a tent in Connemara. The externals could hardly be more different, but it is the same Lord. The appeal of ornament is lessening by the hour in our time, and simplicity is taking its place. Stark plainness can bring about the same sense of awe that once relied on intricate design or elaborate ornament. Inner and outer decor are correlated, inner decor being what we place in our own interiority. Our mental world is so complex that we have to simplify in order to preserve the essences, and this need to simplify is expressed in simple buildings and decor.

If a picture says more than a thousand words, imagine what a building says. It swallows us alive and we are at the mercy of its atmosphere. The places we have associated all our lives with God *are* God for us, as far as they are able to be; they help create or destroy our religious awareness. Some modern architects have worked miracles of design, and I pick out the churches I like as Kawai picked out pots: with the body; I find myself going into them.

Across the face of Ireland – perhaps the world – communities are building prayer-rooms: rooms that are comfortable and have a human scale. They remind me of birds' nests. No doubt the spirit needs both: a church for the Liturgy and a room for private prayer. It echoes the rhythm of the spirit: a "sallying forth" (as Eckhart called it) and a returning.

There is also a lower limit in scale: if strangers are huddled into a small space they escape into themselves and become anonymous to one another like people in a bus. It is not by anyone's decision; it simply happens that way. It is not about packing objects into a space; it is about the interpenetration of spirits. Here in the meditation room there is human space for twenty people or more, but these exuberant twelve seem to fill it.

Someone suggested that we bring along the symbolic objects made during the day and place them before the low altar. (It is in proportion to a meditation stool.) They look surprisingly lovely there. They are on a mat on the ground and this is a final touching humility. Several things together made of unfired clay can look good, while a single one by itself looks very raw. No one refers to them any more and that is better, because it is possible to kill a symbol with too much analysis; then it floats like a dead fish to the top of the mind and becomes a mere idea. These shapes remain a silent expression of one's pain or joy, a *mudra,* expression become expression-to-God.

I have often noticed that the Eucharist picks up what has gone before it; it is like a sponge that absorbs atmosphere and mood. The difficulty with it, usually, is that little or nothing has gone before, and it does not stand – nor was it meant to stand – by itself. Many of the experiences that are made available for us are packaged tidily with no loose ends. Plays, concerts, films, television programmes and, to a lesser extent, football matches are self-enclosed units that make their impact there and then, and do not implicate one's whole life in the way that the Eucharist does. Here, the Eucharist is a natural part of the day; it is usually very quiet and simple and has pools of silence, reflecting the day we have spent together.

The Liturgy of the Word is at the same time a Liturgy of silence; words have to have silence in which to resonate and be heard. The Christian faith puts a strong emphasis on the word: the incarnate Word, the biblical word, the prophetic word, the kerygmatic word. But modern society, equally, is in love with words, for we have torrents of them coming at us day and night, in print and through the air. How can the *Logos*, the sacred word, not be swept away in this flood? *Logos,* indeed, meant more than *word;* it meant the inner principle, the meaning, the inner harmony of something. Even so, it can still be swept away in the flood. The Hebrew word *dabar* meant not only *word* but *event* or *deed,* and this was transmitted in some older translations: "Let us go over to Bethlehem to see this *word* that has come to pass." If *word* has the connotation of *God's deed,* then it is not by speaking but by being profoundly silent and receptive that we allow it to touch our hearts.

We sit in meditation for ten minutes or so and then begin the Eucharist out of this silence. It allows words and actions to have contours, to be seen against a sky of silence. Silence is something one has to wait for, in oneself or in others; it cannot be imposed. It falls like dust: any attempt to hurry it up would only create further disturbance. The wiser self is in tune with the Spirit of God who is gentle and can be frightened away like a small bird at the window.

"We have this treasure in earthen vessels," someone is reading from St Paul. God's Spirit lives in this frail flesh. Even the strongest is easily broken. Exquisite fragility of life, hanging by a gossamer thread: but it is a glory, not a reproach. We tremble, but what is wrong with trembling? The leaves on the trees tremble and they are not ashamed. And music is a kind of trembling. What kind of existence would we have if everything were rock-solid? It would be an intolerable heaviness. In our very trembling we are a musical instrument of God, "showing that the transcendent power belongs to God."

Words fade in the air, leaving something between us, a glow in the heart. The shape of thought is smooth and beautiful, suspended in silence. A dog barking far away, traffic muffled by distance, the sharp cry of a child: the Word of God is spoken to this very world.

O God, you are my God, for you I long;
for you my soul is thirsting.
My body pines for you
like a dry weary land without water.
       Psalm 62:1

This we know: that we long, we thirst, we pine, we are dry and weary – but for *you*, God? If only we could be sure that the deepest meaning of all our longing was God…. We are untidy packages; but when we look at the world of nature we get a hint that God may be a bit untidy too, and likes to frustrate our attempts to become too tidy too soon. O wild God, redeem me from my tame and tidy virtues; convert my heart to love untidy You more than my own timid arrangements. O God, you are not my God at all; you are your own, and to live before you is to feel your gravity that pulls me beyond everything I call *mine*.

Someone has chosen a reading with the sense of touch in mind; it is the passage in Mark's gospel where the woman touched the hem of the Lord's garment and was cured. She sneaked up behind him and tried to sneak away again. We know the temptation to seek an anonymous solution to personal problems, to search for abstract redemption under names like *peace, adjustment, fulfilment.* There is a blind reaching out for anything that will help us to cope. But what a shattering of anonymous relation-ships in these three words, "who touched me?" He did not come that we might be able to cope; he came that we might have life in abundance.

We bring bread and wine and speak words over them to God our Father – three worlds alienated from one another: *nature, language* and *God.* But only here are they at one again. Here language is *logos.* It may be clothed in a Cork accent but it is the inner meaning of this bread and wine. We are not, in Hesse's phrase, "alienated from nature and hanging suspended in space", for our *logos* is the *logos* of the world. And God is speaking in these words.

"The passion and death of Christ belong to us as fully as if we had suffered them ourselves." I must have read this in Thomas Aquinas years ago as I crammed for exams in theology, but it failed to strike root in the mind's weed-patch. Having rediscovered it, I think of little else at Mass. Christ is our brother: the Father cannot see us apart from him. So we stand before our Father with pride and joy, not in tortured anxiety.

The Eucharist makes its own silence; we do not make it.... Even on bad days a sense of the unconditional penetrates. Here is a space clear of the word *if*. *If is* the meanest word in the English language. If it were a person instead of a word what would it look like? It would be pale and tight-lipped, crippled with caution, cold, joyless, worried and calculating. On bad days a person can look just like the word *if*. When I have a moment of inner freedom and I am tempted to risk speaking to a stranger or hugging a friend or giving away something that is valuable to me, *if* arrives to cripple me; *if* wants nothing to happen, good or bad. How could there be any *ifs* in God our Father's love?

There is softness in people's faces. The body makes the mind and spirit visible. It is astonishing how *visible* everything is; all one has to do is look. Look without thinking, as a child does, and the inner and outer worlds become one. There are people with square jaws who talk about God and have hearts of stainless steel. When someone mentions God to me I no longer listen to what he or she is saying; I watch the set of the jaw; I watch the eyes. I want to *see* God. God is love. The absence of love in a person is as plain as the nose on your face. A man or woman whose main driving force in life is competition, or envy, or escape, or having power over others, simply cannot speak about God. "The one who does not love does not know God, for God is love."

Communion, too, is in silence. It has its own power, and there is no gap that needs to be filled in with singing. This kind of filling in is just fear of silence and a disbelief in the Eucharist as an *action*. Sometimes the power of the action itself strikes me with a vivid freshness. We do not normally feed one another so directly as this, nor drink from the same cup or glass. It is about giving and receiving in a total way despite the miserly appearance of the altar breads.

There was once a miser who fell into a well. All the people in the village gathered around the mouth of the well and wanted to haul him out, but it was proving impossible, for when anyone reached down and shouted, "Give me your hand!" the habit of a lifetime made the miser recoil at the sound of the word *give*. But a man came from the back of the crowd, reached down and shouted, "Take my hand!" Immediately the miser grabbed it and was hauled to safety! There is no difference between giving and receiving – except for a miser. Not only the receiver but the giver also is enriched in giving. The greatest stagnation is when others no longer receive from me; soon I cease to have anything to give. Even in such ordinary exchanges as handshakes or hugs, it is artificial to distinguish giver and receiver. They are in communion.

It took an old pagan to show me how specific the Christian vision of giving and receiving is. There is something chilling about Aristotle's description of the superior person who likes to confer benefits, because this implies superiority, but hates to receive them, because this implies inferiority. When such a one repays a service it is with interest, "for in this way the original benefactor will become the beneficiary and debtor in turn." And another mark of the superior person is "his refusal or reluctance to ask anyone to help him, while always ready to bring help himself." I often forget how chilly the ancient pagan world was – in its highest aspirations, at any rate. (On the ground it was probably as torrid as anywhere else.) The higher their philosophies soared the chillier they became (with the exception of Plato's).

I know a few people who, like Aristotle's superior man, are unable to ask for help or receive a gift. If you help them in any way, even inadvertently, they wait to get you back. They are superficially the friendliest people, but they are unable to endure mutuality. It takes a certain humility and freedom to receive from one another and from God. Most of the doctrines of the Christian faith are about *receiving* graciously: existence, grace, the Spirit, the Eucharist.. ... This is the dearest thing we give to God, our receptivity; for giving and receiving are profoundly one, as all opposites are one.

At one moment I become aware again of the clay shapes on the floor between us. Their variety conveys a sense of the individuality of our presence to one another and to God. The comical way they seem to huddle together reminds me of day-old chicks. What a funny mystery is community! Some of the most beautiful pots in the world are full of technical defects. Japanese *raku* tea-bowls, treasured in museums, even retain the marks made by the tongs on the molten glaze as they were drawn from the kiln. This teaches me to treasure differences and not to reject people on technicalities. Let perfect people – if there are any – band together for their own purposes; Christian community is for people who know their own weaknesses. It is this admission that makes it possible for us, as it was not possible for Aristotle's superior man, to laugh at ourselves. Aristotle was no company for anyone, but Jesus made saints out of the likes of us. As a young man he had read Ezekiel with flaming eyes:

> The weak you have not strengthened, the sick you have not healed, the crippled you have not bound up, the strayed you have not brought back, the lost you have not sought, and with force and harshness you have ruled them. (34:4)

Years later he told a story about a lost sheep and ninety-nine safe ones; and the irony of it is that the ninety-nine are an optical illusion. Every man and woman is the lost sheep.

At this Eucharist, Aristotle's superior man is haunting me. (John Wayne transmitted something of him to all of us!) His greatest sadness must have been the inability to be *thankful*. If I have no deep sense of thanksgiving I am locked within the rigid boundaries of a narrow *idea* of self. But the full self is a gently unfolding world that celebrates its joyful Eucharist to a warm God.

We have reached the end and the moment of detachment. These retreats we call *The Potter* seem to bring people very close to one another, probably for the same reason that we feel close to childhood friends: we have laughed and cried and played and prayed together. As I take leave of my friends and they take leave of one another, a thought recurs: that we describe *separation* too prosaically. We say things like, "So-and-so is going home because he has to collect his friend from work." If the world has no magic for us it is our own fault. There is so much meeting and parting in our lives that they must surely produce more feeling in us than the reading of a time-table. My friends did not arrive on the number 8 bus; they came from the invisible, manifested themselves, and they have returned to the invisible.

7

Fact and Fiction

Time is a child
Moving pointers in a game;
The royal power is a child's.
    Heraclitus

It is three days before Christmas and no one wants to make a retreat or get dirty hands or create symbols. In this season the symbols are ready-made and venerable. A friend asks if she could bring a pre-school class to meet Santa Claus in the Mews. The place has an unusual atmosphere and might well match a child's idea of a village where everything is magic and toys. She waits till I have absorbed this and said yes; then she unfolds her plan a little more: I am to be Santa Claus!

We love to study life's stages and turning-points, and without doubt there will soon be a psychological study of the first time one is asked to be Santa Claus. It makes you check your age, your girth, your seriousness as a citizen. I list the objections: I have neither the age nor the girth, so my lack of seriousness must be my only qualification. These objections are quickly disposed of: to a four-year-old every adult is an eternal being; and pillows can make up what nature has not supplied. I even have one positive attribute: a beard.

THEY ARRIVE, an unmistakeable group, chains of them holding hands. Small children in a group always make me think of a crop of some kind. These are in bunches, like bananas, and they stare with huge eyes at everything. I am watching them from my hiding place, feeling fat and foolish in my red outfit. There is a hall that was once a coach-house, and they file in. I am to emerge from the Hermitage at a signal and make a rumbustious entrance, but not so rumbustious as to scare them. My friend's husband was rejected for the role after last Christmas when his powerful laugh scared their predecessors out of their wits. I make my way with a pre-arranged sack of labelled surprises. I can hear their amazement as I come into view, and I can also see some of it: that is, to a distance of about ten feet, for I have had to leave my glasses behind. Santa Clauses are expected to have 20/20 vision for seeing how good everybody is. But in fact it works equally well at the other extreme: there is a kind of generalised goodwill that comes from being able to see very little. I know a priest who always removes his glasses, for this reason, when he is preaching.

I tell them several stories and their attention is total – certainly that of the ones within ten feet of me. Gradually I am aware that the role is strangely familiar. After half an hour I know who I am: I am a priest of the forties or fifties. I have unearned attention; there is even a touch of awe. I am visually unmistakeable and my place in society is unquestioned by myself or anyone else. In a way, my personal qualities count for little; no matter how much less than a man I may be, I am still more than a man, for the role is bigger than the actor, as the pillows remind me. Like a young Santa Claus I play tricks with time: I have no age of my own, for I am called 'Father' by people twice my age. I look out myopically at a world of 'children' whose love for me would suddenly turn to fear if I raised my voice. When they come to me I must make a show of familiarity and goodwill and say words that have been said a thousand times before. Here in the Mews, three days before Christmas, the role still exists in perfect working order and delights a group of four-year-olds.

There is a bright-eyed being sitting on my knee and testing my authenticity for herself by tugging at my beard. I fail the test, for she announces, "You're not a real Santy!" I am astonished at the way her challenge fills me with anxiety as I hurry to weed out this heresy. "How can you say that?" I probe. "Because your beard doesn't come off," she says quite simply, and turns her attention to the parcel bearing her name that I have ready in my hand. I am being taught something new about fact and fiction by this radical atom on my knee. It shows how dangerous it is to patronise children. They are the real experts at distinguishing fantasy and reality. They take fantasy with deadly seriousness, but this does not mean that they confuse it with reality.

Now that she has lifted one corner of my falsity she warms to her task. She is comparing me with the poster of a much more authentic Santa Claus on the wall. He is everything that a Santa Claus should be: red-cheeked, pudgy and old. "You're not like the Santy on the wall," she says, coming in for another attack. It is difficult when your reality is denied by someone who is sitting on your knee. I did not expect to have to think at all – let alone think fast – in this role. "That's a photograph of me when I was older," I tell her, and to my surprise and relief it satisfies her. They live in a timeless world where experiences are distinguished by intensity and not by chronology. *We* live by the clock and so we have the impression that the past is simply past and the future simply future. But a child is closer to the live experience of time. The past may be so powerful in a person that nothing else seems real; or the future may so possess someone that past and present are nothing.

A tiny girl stands straight in front of me (within range), staring with her head forward. Then she begins to jump up and down in a kind of ecstasy. It takes possession of her and she laughs and dances in complete self-forgetfulness. I have never seen anyone so possessed by joy. It is a glimpse of God's kind of life; and the knowledge that I have been the occasion of it is a great comfort after the inquisition her friend has put me through. How can we believe that God's life is bliss and that that life is poured out in us, and yet never dance to God? I have a beautiful friend who after a long time of sadness found herself one day spontaneously yielding to this kind of dance, and it became a major pivot-point of her life. Look at us in church, priest and people alike; we look walled-in; we feel rigid and dead. There are invisible chains and manacles everywhere. This kind of rigidity holds a special horror for me and when I see it beginning to appear in a retreat-group during a session, I say or do something a little crazy to set them (and myself) free. In serious cases I have made impersonal, spine-chilling howls, like someone who has been shot with an arrow in the back. Or I have collapsed on the floor as if dead (this has a very enlivening effect on a group). And for milder cases I have sometimes continued exactly as before but with a sudden and complete loss of sound. I have noticed that people always remain alert when they are unable to predict what will happen next. There is little point in going through a charade of mutual imprisonment; that is how people come to hate life. This tiny girl would not be allowed to dance like this in church.

A boy with dead eyes comes up when I read his name on the parcel. He does not see me at all but makes a grab for the gift. It is an ugly impersonal action, but it is undisguised. We see plainly in children the best and the worst that is hidden in ourselves. There are many suave people who are greedier than this boy, but they manage to camouflage it. I push the parcel inside my red outfit, where there is little room for it because of pillows. Now, at least, he has to deal with me. What crimes have been committed against this child that a box of crayons can make Santa Claus invisible to him? What has happened already to his sense of wonder? How will he ever dance for joy or come to know God? At his age the deepest layer of his experience is being laid down, and it is an impersonal greed. He begins to poke at my chest as if it were a cupboard. I blow in his ear, and when he looks at me I haul him onto my lap and talk to him; but he sits there in passive resistance. I know when I am out of my depth and I let him go with his crayons.

Here comes another one with blond ringlets and a melting smile. She makes it clear from the start that she intends to take me over. This, in adult form, would be the most challenging of all, for how could you retain your own reality without appearing a brute? A human being is at once too little and too much to be taken over: too little, because no human being will ever fulfil another; and too much, because you need to stand in your own reality. Will this little beauty spend her life taking people over, or is this the early phase of a healthy emotional life? I realise how little I know about love and its stages. My friend leads her away but she is back in a minute with a confidence about her Daddy, beaming her smile with deadly accuracy. The culmination is when she tells me she loves me. Think of the power this statement will have in twenty years' time! What floundering male could resist it? I have always naively thought that love and power were opposites, but today my education is being extended.

By now the floor is covered with wrapping paper and there is yellow and red plastic everywhere and brightly covered colouring-books. It was plastic that drove me to carpentry years ago, to make wooden toys for my nephews and nieces. Wood is a friendly substance: it has colour and warmth and a smell and texture of its own. Its history is written in the grain and you can always imagine it as the tree it once was, moving in the wind and being a home to hundreds of small creatures. But plastic seems almost alien to this planet: it has no colour or texture of its own, no real smell; it is neither warm like wood nor cold like metal. You cannot even get rid of it: it has not the decency to decay when it is no longer needed. Yet it is sometimes used to simulate flowers, the most fragile things in the world. These 'flowers' never die, for the good reason that they have never been alive. They have the kind of awful immortality that Swift imagined on one of Gulliver's islands.

Once on an Ash Wednesday it struck me what a startling thing it is to daub people's foreheads with ashes. Most religions make a big thing of washing, cleansing, purifying. Baptism, in some respects, follows this pattern, but Ash Wednesday makes a mess. I was daubing a rich-looking lady who wore heavy make-up when I became aware that ashes and make-up are exact opposites. Make-up says: I am not involved in the process of ageing, the wind and the weather do not touch me, I am as immortal as plastic. The daub of ashes says the opposite: admit I am fragile, vulnerable, mortal. These, and not make-up, are some of the qualities that make people beautiful.

Make-up and toiletries are often advertised with the promise that they will restore your youthful appearance, will give you the soft skin and clear eyes of these children. The cult of youth and youthfulness in these times looks like a strong affirmation of life, but it is actually a philosophy of despair. Everyone's youth is slipping away, minute by minute, inexorably, even that of these four-year-olds. A real affirmation of life would be a cult of old age, as in traditional Japan. There the meaning of life was in its fulfilment and not in its first flush. In our despairing times we love the acorn and hate the oak. We pursue what someone called an 'inverted Confucianism': we worship our grandchildren.

Age is a matter of perspective, in any case. If you sit on an imaginary fence (which you cannot do) and watch your life passing by, you see yourself getting older every minute. This is the usual perspective. If, however, you situate yourself *within* your life (which you cannot but do), you are actually getting *younger* all the time, and your far-off childhood is the oldest part of you. An image will make it clearer: Imagine that you are sitting on a fence watching a mountain stream at its source. Now imagine, instead, that you *are* the mountain stream. The water that first bubbled out of the ground in this place many years ago is now far away in the valley and is the 'oldest' part of the stream. The youngest is the water that is bubbling up this instant. If we keep our attention on the present instant (which is the only instant there is) we are eternally young. Because we lose touch with our own eternal youth, we project it onto children. But it is wasted on them, as someone said, for they never appreciate it. They are not young, they are timeless.

I am drawn out of my reverie by a very small fair-haired lad who comes with long strides and takes his place on my knee without as much as by my leave. This is a talker, who takes an interest in the details of things. Do I live here? "Yes, some of the time." (I want to leave room for the North Pole.) Am I married? "No … no." (Why not a celibate Santa Claus? Why leave it all to priests?) They have a Parkray at home and it has only a skinny chimney, and they have a burglar-alarm on the doors and windows; how will I get in? "Magic!" (No harm to stretch his empiricist mind a little.) What do I do for the rest of the year? "It's always Christmas somewhere in the world." (This is a difficult notion and actually untrue, but let him cut his teeth on it.) I wonder how long the myth of Santa Claus can withstand this kind of mind. Today he is investigating Santa Claus, tomorrow the parish priest.

I know a scrupulous priest who told a churchful of children one Christmas that Santa Claus did not exist. What a killjoy! Faith is in greater danger from a dead imagination than from a living one. Its deepest truths are transmitted in the form of poetry, myth, story. But there is a narrow literal attitude that would reduce all this luxuriant expression to a kind of crossword puzzle, where there is only one right word in every case. Living with faith demands great imaginative and sympathetic leaps throughout one's life, and if we become too factual about it we may miss it altogether. Children understand hidden forms better than we do; they love to disguise themselves and act out the realities that touch them. I have yet to meet one who was disillusioned by the unmasking of Santa Claus – unless he or she had already been given reason for disillusionment with the whole adult world.

Santa Claus does not hang around; if he did he would lose his mystery. It is very important to know when something is over. There is a point beyond which there is nothing but diminishing returns, and to know when this point is reached is one of the most difficult arts. Most of our experiences leave us back at square one for want of the discipline of this art. My friend has perceived this finishing-point and nods at me to go. Thin as a rake within my bulging pillows, a poor relation of Aldous Huxley's fat and loving aunt, I wave them expansive goodbyes, promising to return on Christmas night. And I will indeed, for lexical accuracy is only half the truth.

8

Solitude and Community

Nothing falls any longer into deep wells. Everything among them speaks, nothing prospers and comes to an end any longer. Everything cackles, but who still wants to sit quietly upon the nest and hatch eggs? … Everything among them speaks, everything is betrayed. O humankind, you strange thing!
  Nietzsche

One of the most stinging things in Nietzsche is his insistence on putting himself apart from the human race. His is a solitude too remote and cold, for he does not love us enough. If he is "breathing the air of a solitary peak," it is not because he has gone forth to fight some arduous battle on our behalf, but because he cannot endure our company for long. The solitude of Jesus, who came from the desert and whose custom it was to spend nights on the mountain or climb up there long before dawn, has a different quality.

The Spirit drove him out into the wilderness, and he was in the wilderness forty days, tempted by Satan; and he was with the wild beasts. (Mark 1:12)

In the Bible the desert was the abode of demons and wild beasts, but it was also the place where one might meet God. Israel first met God in the desert, and the story of their forty years of wandering through the desert remains a parable of the meeting of humankind with God. It has been said that whoever delights in solitude is either a wild beast or a god. One could agree this far: whoever delights in solitude will *meet* one or the other, more likely both. The wild beasts of the desert symbolise the wild beasts within the self that have to be faced on the journey to God.

I cannot reach any depth in my life unless I pass many times through a *desert experience,* an experience of solitude, of separation from society and the many false identities it imposes. I have to breathe the air of a solitary peak. It is a stepping into possession of my own being and destiny with God. So many people claim to own me; from the cradle I am smothered with possessive pronouns: *our* baby, *my* son, *my* friend…. Even Jesus had to struggle against false identities. When he climbed a mountain in the evening or the early morning and remained there in mysterious contact with his Father, all easy identities were left far below. He was not the family boy, the village lad, the son of Joseph, or a worldly leader…. It must be in moments like this that he became aware that "I and the Father are one." That was his deepest identity.

Like Nietzsche's Zarathustra, he descended from the mountain into society, but what a different coming-down: "I am weary of my wisdom," said Zarathustra, "like a bee that has gathered too much honey; I need hands outstretched to take it." Despite his saying so, Zarathustra does not love us; he came down to lecture us, for his own relief; he is cold and impersonal. But there was nothing cold or impersonal about Jesus.

Here in the Mews there is a place of solitude where many have done battle with their wild beasts and searched for God. It is the little house known as the Hermitage.

In the days when Ennismore was owned by the gentry, the Mews was only a mews – that is, stables, coach-houses and the coachman's house. It had none of the romance that clings like ivy to old walls. Romance is something we attach to old buildings long after their use has been forgotten, or at least after it has become sufficiently remote for all memories of hardship to have faded. I find it saddening to imagine all the nameless coachmen and their nameless wives and children who lived here since 1824, while the big family traced its ancestry to the Middle Ages. This is the only romance it holds for me: a sadness for all the humble human stories that are lost forever. In a way, the coachman's house has always been a Hermitage.

It took nine months of my spare time to restore this building. Only when the work was finished did I see a connection between this old house and the fact that I have been dreaming since childhood, sometimes almost nightly, of derelict houses. It is a shock when you ask yourself, with some evidence to hand, whether your waking life might be only a reflection of your dream life. However, a waking life that was not in some sense the outcome of a dream would be a very boring one. You must give birth to your images, as Rilke expressed it, for they are the future waiting to be born; "the future must enter into you long before it happens."

This nine-month (or life-long) gestation has been fruitful for the hundreds of people who have prayed in the tiny prayer-room, or sat alone in reverie before the fire, tasting the joy and terror of solitude. If we ask which side of our nature, more than another, is being made invisible in today's world, we can fairly readily say: the need of every person for solitude. All the ills of the world, it has been said, stem from our being unable to sit still in solitude for five minutes.

But it is becoming increasingly difficult to find space that is not filled up with noise or talk or music. Wherever human beings have been, of course, there has been noise, but the new element in our age is systematic inattention. We use music, or even speech, as a kind of 'wallpaper', not to engage our attention but to alleviate silence and stillness. This is an invention of our century, and it caused dismay when it was first introduced in a Paris theatre sometime in the early decades. The people began to return to their seats when light music was played during the intermission, and the manager had to come on stage and instruct them not to listen. But systematic inattention is now second nature to us.

I sometimes experience in myself this urge to fill up all the chinks with noise and activity. It is a way of avoiding one's life. One of the great sages of ancient China, Chuang – Tzu, told a story about a man who was alarmed at his own shadow, which followed him everywhere (and this was long before Jung!), and at his own footsteps. He decided to run away from them all; but they kept pace with him effortlessly. Seeing this, he ran faster and faster till he finally fell dead from exhaustion. He should have sat down in the shade, Chuang-Tzu said, and there would have been no shadow and no more footsteps. I am that fleeing man. If I run from my solitude I can expect to be running forever. One clear insight into the absurdity of it is enough. I have to face everything that is in the self. To avoid the full self and try to live with only a few parts, is also to avoid God who wants the whole heart, the whole soul, the whole strength, the whole mind.

I have long since lost count of the people who have stayed in the Hermitage. There have been people, young and old, from every walk of life; and in all that number there was only one who physically fled from the solitude. I am quite certain that it is not a fad or a fancy. It is easy and amusing to play at being a hermit for a day or two, living on dry bread and making a show of being ascetical. Even if there is no-one else to see the show, the self is audience enough; and it loves a romantic distraction from ordinary life. But in this Hermitage, solitude is the only asceticism; it is the most essential asceticism of our time. Very few people are capable of fasting (for instance) for a genuine spiritual motive. It is too like too many other things: dieting, slimming, system-cleansing, self-sufficiency.... But a solitude that is not 'filled in' with acting or experimentation brings us face to face with the fleeing self and consequently with God.

I have often wished that this house could be a Hermitage for me too, but sadly it cannot. The moment I step inside the door I become a maintenance man. Once or twice a year a longer period of solitude becomes a matter of urgency for me; I drop out of circulation for a few days and live in a tent in a forest twenty miles away.

Someone once wrote about "the two hands of God." By this he meant all the opposites of the world: solitude and community, joy and sorrow, giving and receiving, work and rest, speech and silence....On the surface these opposites look like enemies, but there is a profound interdependence. Someone who cannot endure solitude has nothing to bring to community, and someone who cannot endure community is only further reduced by solitude. "There are some solitary wretches," said Alexander Pope, "who seem to have left the rest of mankind only as Eve left Adam, to meet the devil in private." In less negative language, the more fully I enter solitude, the more creatively I can live with people later on; and the deeper my relationships with others in community, the less 'sticky' I will be and the more capable of real solitude. "With every creature," said Eckhart, "according to the nobility of its nature, the more it indwells in itself, the more it gives itself out."

Solitude, when one enters it, gives a deep quality, a mellow quietness and solidity. There is a superficiality and faintness about a person who cannot be alone. If I find my meaning only in others, then when I am alone I will have a painful sense of meaninglessness. I will run to others to find myself, or I will run to others to lose myself. But what then if I should find that the others are running too? "Loneliness," said Paul Tillich, "can only be conquered by those who can bear solitude."

S HE LOOKED diffident as she arrived with her bag, glancing around as if to check that she was not trespassing. I show her where I have been splitting blocks of timber for the fire, and she begins to look more at ease. She has been under the stress of a difficult home life and feels spent, she explains; she feels lost to the Lord too, and hopes that three or four days here will give her spirit time to find its own pace again. We enter the Hermitage and once more I see the easing effect that its simplicity has on people. She makes straight for the centre, which is a tiny prayer-room, and settles herself there. She would like to remain there for ten or fifteen minutes, while I light the fire in the study.

I have noticed that every house has a centre. Even when the architecture does nothing to create one, a centre arises spontaneously. I once lived in a very large randomly-built priory which had no architectural centre; even the kitchen, often the spontaneous centre, was unhomely. A centre sprouted nearby, however, at the last table in the large dining-room. It was at that table that all the best conversations took place, often late at night, for the centre of a house is the place people feel they have to visit, however briefly and ritually, when they come home. The location of this tiny prayer-room in the Hermitage was a happy accident. It is at the very centre of the house, as if by design. So it had the combined advantages of accident and design: it looks inevitable.

When she emerges she indicates that she would like to talk for a while, so we sit for an hour by the fire. It is her enslavement to other people's expectations that has drained her of her power, she says. We must try to understand how this enslavement happens. Is it possible to trace the fault? Perhaps it has to do, like so many things, with an uncertainty about one's own identity. If I have some weight of my own I will not be pulled so easily into someone else's orbit. If I know who I am I will also know who I am not, and so I will be able to say 'no' to other people's demands when that is appropriate. I have to place my 'no'-signals on the map and be prepared to be out of favour till people become used to them.

I have a very alive and sage friend who, for years, has known how this is done. She has made her grown-up family aware of her need for personal space by inventing her own word for it. She has trained them to expect a "growly day" every four or five weeks: she tells them that they will be on their own and can sink or swim according to preference, while she spends the day by the sea or going for a long walk or sitting under a tree in the countryside. They have never sunk yet. I tell my 'hermit' about this friend, and her eyes sparkle with a resolution that will probably draw loud protests at home if she has the courage to put it into practice. Why, she asks herself, must she come to the verge of a breakdown before she can take time for herself? We use ourselves as we would use a machine. We drive ourselves as hard as we can go, and we stop only when there is a breakdown. She refers to her body as it, and for the first time this strikes me as odd. Why do we not say *he* or *she*? *It* is good enough for a machine or for a dead body, but it is hardly good enough for a living one. There is a kind of unease with the self that gives us, first, a bad conscience, and then a harshness, towards the body.

She is determined to exercise compassion on herself (not too much determination, I hope, and not too much exercising.) She picks up the book in which her predecessors have written prayers and poems during their time here. These writings have accumulated over a few years and they never fail to touch my heart, born as they are out of solitude and prayer. Some are diffuse and preachy, some are small and bright as a button, one or two are in the style of Japanese haiku. But all are heart-felt, and they create a sort of tenuous tradition, which began and grew spontaneously when I left this book here by a lucky mistake.

Lord, you have let me experience fear and loneliness in my life; but they have helped me to know what it is like to trust you.

Dogs barking in the distance.
In this room the fire
Is murmuring to me of friends.

I think of all who have been alone here.
Alone here, I feel at one
with people I have never met.

I am not listening:
I hear only my own answers.

Thank you, God my Father, for yesterday evening
when I suddenly knew that you were with me.

"Will I be afraid," she wonders, "when the night falls?" Many people have never spent a night alone in a house. The massive gates and locks in the Mews do not fully relieve this fear, for it has roots that go deep into the self. It is simply something that we have to face, and if we face it with awareness it has much to teach us. Whistling in the dark is a wrong method; its very first step is in the wrong direction: it is a denial of the truth that we are afraid. I have found that the only way to cope with fear is to admit that I am afraid, see my fear just as it is and decide to value the new sharpness of the senses that it produces in me. Fear can become neurotic, but it is not itself a neurosis. It is a natural instinct, so it cannot be simply an enemy or a problem. Its purpose is to make us more alert, and if we try to arrange our lives in such a way that we seldom have to experience it, the penalty is an all-pervading dullness and boredom.

She has the keys of the Hermitage and of the big gates; she knows about the 'mile-walk' in the grounds; she is welcome at community Liturgy in the main retreat centre if she wants it. I have nothing to do now but get out of her way and leave her to do battle with her demons and wild beasts, and to meet the Lord who said: "I will lead you into solitude and there I will speak to your heart." (Hosea 2:14)

9

Fire and Clay

This world was ever, is now, and ever shall be an ever-living Fire, with measures of it kindling and measures of it going out.
    Heraclitus

The ancient Greeks brooded on the four elements: fire, air, earth, water. But the heavenly bodies, they believed, had to be made of material that was purer than these earthly essences, so they called it 'the fifth essence', *quinta essentia* (from which we get the word 'quintessence'). They did not realise that the earth was a heavenly body and that it was as pure as anything that could be found. Of course the number of elements that scientists now speak of exceeds a hundred, but at the everyday level these ancient four are always with us. It struck me once that the making of pottery involves all four of these ancient elements: clay is from the earth, it contains water, dries in the air, and it is fired to red or white-hot temperatures in a kiln.

There must be a sense in which it is more natural for a human being to work with these elements than to work in advertising, income tax or banking. Many who make the six-day summer retreats in the Mews are people in these and similar professions who feel the need to return to the sanity of nature and the self and God. Travel companies certainly recommend a return to nature, but only to certain patches of it that are about a thousand miles from where we are. These three – nature, the self, and God – are wherever we are, and returning to them is a skill that is being stripped from us by many influences in modern life.

Before these retreats begin I try to spend a few days potting. This has a strong healing effect after too much talk, for preachers usually suffer from having said too much. Speech causes bad faith unless it comes from one's deepest centre. Here at the wheel, my centre of gravity can move southwards from the head – and in particular from the mouth!

I am preparing for *The Potter-2*. This is a six-day retreat for second-timers. I am lucky enough to have gifted friends who spend their gifts prodigally for the twenty people who come to each of these retreats. We use many methods, as the interests of the group demand: drawing, yoga, movement, as well as work with clay. I keep the Hermitage free for this week, and it becomes a further resource. It is good to have an annual excuse to pull out all the stops!

It is odd to speak of a 'retreat team'; there is an urge to continue the metaphor and imagine them prancing on to the field in their colours. We would be a droll team: a yogi, an artist and a potter. Even if we do not use the word 'team', we are able to work together without confusion or the uptightness that excessive planning causes. The objection to 'team' is that it makes all the others spectators, and that is precisely what our twenty friends are not.

Being second-timers they arrive with strong boots and ample aprons. Clay, like soil, creates unspoken partnerships, and I feel at ease in this clay-spattered boiler-suit. They lose no time in making themselves at home, beaming at every object as if it were an old friend. It is a relief not to feel I should make excuses for the dirtiness of clay; I never make them, but the feeling itself is uncomfortable. A pottery workshop, and the things in it, should not be filthy but they can never be spotless; the best that can be hoped for is a reasonable compromise between the two. Many people spend their lives sterilising their surroundings and persecuting spiders, but for what purpose? We ourselves return to this same earth in the end, so we might as well make friends with it now. (As solid evidence, a nearby convent, whose corridors were waxed and polished daily by generations of novices, now lies mouldering.) But already these twenty make it clear that they intend to live this week with the four elements.

A man whose distinctive humour I remember is sitting on the stone trough in the courtyard, signalling and telling his soul aloud that it is safe to come home now. Thank God for clowns: they enable the rest of us to dare to be human, to shed in some measure what Nietzsche called 'the Spirit of Gravity'.

"And when I beheld my devil, I found him to be serious, thorough, profound, solemn: it was the Spirit of Gravity."

But Gravity we always thought good, and Levity bad. Levity was obscene in the literal sense: it was 'off-stage', just a skit in the wings, while the main show was a joyless grind. I think now we should learn to enjoy ourselves more, for this is the best way to unlearn how to do evil to others and kill their joy. I recall my student days in Switzerland when the highest word of commendation for a book – or a lecturer, or indeed anything whatsoever – was *serieux*; and this was always accompanied by facial expressions of gravity, comical in twenty-year-olds. Years later I was told that the key word was now *solide*. I am grateful for this clown on the water-trough; he has an unusual gift: the ability to laugh at himself. Every country makes jokes about some smaller country or about some group within itself: the Canadians about Newfoundlanders, Italians about Sicilians, the English about the Irish, and the Irish about Kerry people. This is due to an inability to laugh at oneself, or at least to the greater ease there is in laughing at others. This clown, if his charm lasts, will help us to exorcise the Spirit of Gravity; then we may catch a glimpse of the other Spirit, who has been likened to Fire.

As our number grows towards the fulness of twenty we hear many horror stories about potting in kitchens, firing in cookers, piles of clay in garages, clay hardened into sitting-room carpets. There are good stories too: of meditation, of the way of compassion, of God experienced afresh. One woman tells us with enthusiasm that she has learnt to do the wash-up without hating it, and that it has even become a kind of meditation for her.

This time we intend to commit some pots and pieces to the fire. This is the most dramatic side of pottery, because fire is the most dramatic of the elements. Fire is the most profound and rapid transformation in nature, and so it has become a metaphor for all that is radical, final, unconstrained. It has been called "a terrible divinity."

Yesterday I went begging for reject bricks to a nearby building-site. As I hauled them home in my wheel-barrow I reflected that these rejects had been tried by fire and found wanting. They will meet fire again, but in a different capacity: they will be the kiln that strives to contain the terrible divinity. A friend who is an expert in these matters is already building the raku kiln in the courtyard, and she is surrounded by twenty wide-eyed adults. We could have decided to use the electric kilns in my own workshop, but this rudimentary kiln will allow a more direct involvement with fire. On the outside it looks like a casual pile of red bricks, but it is lined with ceramic fibre on the inside, and it has all its essential parts: a grate, a firing chamber and a rudimentary chimney. As with every fire, the skill lies in getting the proper draught. Seldom has any builder had twenty assistants. Everyone wants to help, because fire is able to exercise a special magic even before it is visible.

When the kiln is more or less completed (raku kilns are like that), we work for an hour or two with clay. This brings down an atmosphere of quietness and reflection to balance the extroversion of the previous hour. This time we work with groggy clay – potters' language for coarse, gritty clay that can withstand the thermal shocks of raku firing. In the workshop it is pleasantly cool and the clay feels cool to the touch. Clay is silent and real, but we are full of words. It is good to return to this most solid of the elements and the most imprisoned by gravity. We need to experience our own density in order to enliven it from within. Shapes appear on the tables, but when I look again they have changed to other shapes. It is a process that has some of the freedom of water. This is not surprising, because clay is stone in a semi-liquid state. My twenty friends remember what they learned before: not to be imprisoned by the things they make. As I notice their freedom I reflect that the Spirit of Gravity is not in the clay but in ourselves, and that the real prison is the mind alone.

"The distance between you and God is the distance between you and yourself," I quote some holy man to them. If you live through your real self (which God made) and not through your ego (which you yourself made, in collusion with society), you will be living with God. Well then, if these primitive elements – fire, air, earth, water – restore us to ourselves, they will also restore us to God. Besides, they do it by themselves, if we handle them with reverence. There and then we devise a meditation in which we handle the clay with this kind of awareness. We need to straighten out a bias that has placed an intense limitation on our vision: the bias towards the mental. It is not only through our minds and wills that we draw near to God, but through the whole creation:

> If there were no search for God, the heavens themselves would not be revolving. Whether you like it or not, whether you know it or not, secretly all nature seeks God and works towards him. Covertly nature seeks, hunts, tries to ferret out the track on which God may be found.
>
> Meister Eckhart

WE HAVE been talking about these things, and now we fall silent. The way they settle themselves with their lumps of clay reminds me of children going to sleep on the lap. We have a great longing for inner peace; and the strength of this longing is probably a measure of our lack of it. We are complex and we quickly turn it into a love of sleep or even death. One can get too much of "Be still and know that I am God." We certainly need to learn how to be still, yet tension is necessary in the personality, for personality is dynamic and creative. We would be in a sad state if we always got the kind of inner peace we prayed for. I look around at my friends, wondering if I have only helped them to sleep. I tell them this story, just in case....

An Emperor had two artists in his court, and there was bitter rivalry between them. One day the Emperor said, "I want to decide, once for all, which of you is the better artist. You have always chosen opposite themes, because you are jealous of each other; this time, paint the same theme, so that I can judge. And let the theme be 'Peace'." A week later the first artist presented his canvas. It showed a dreamy landscape with rolling hills and a peaceful lake without a ripple on the surface. Looking at this mellow picture, the Emperor even began to feel drowsy. Later the second artist presented his work. It showed a thundering waterfall; one could almost hear the roar of the water as it crashed onto the rocks, hundreds of feet below. "But this is not on the theme of peace, as I ordered," said the Emperor angrily. The artist made no reply but motioned him to continue looking. By and by the Emperor spotted a detail that he had overlooked at first: among the rocks at the base of the waterfall there was a small shrub. And when he peered at it he saw that there was a bird's nest in its branches. Now he became absorbed in it and soon he was able to see, though the detail was minute, that there was a bird in the nest: a sparrow sitting on her eggs, her eyes half-closed; she was waiting for her chicks to be born, a perfect picture of peace. The Emperor raised himself and said: "I thank you, my friend; you have taught me something of tremendous importance about peace. But you," he said, addressing the first artist, "you succeeded only in putting me to sleep."

This story leads to a conversation about conflicts in one's life. "There is no such thing as a life without conflicts," says the quiet man with an effort. We cannot eliminate conflict from our lives, but we can turn destructive conflicts into constructive ones. The crossfire of opposite emotions and drives is ambivalent in itself (as all fire is): it can be good or bad; it can create and destroy. Fire, as Bachelard said, is not only "a terrible divinity" but a tutelary one:

> It shines in Paradise. It burns in Hell. It is gentleness and torture. It is cookery and it is apocalypse. It is a tutelary and terrible divinity, both good and bad.

Meditating with clay, as we are doing now, is not an escape into a peaceful little patch, aside from life; it is a simplified situation in which the shape of our whole life may become clear. We may catch a glimpse of some destructive energy in ourselves and be set free, in this atmosphere, to allow that energy to transform itself into compassion. Energy is indestructible; it can only be transformed. The destroying fires may yet be transformed into warm love.

We have been drifting back and forth between silence and conversation. An old friend begins to reflect aloud on the difference between *change* and *transformation*. Change is an external manipulation; transformation is from within, like growth. We try to change ourselves as we would change an inanimate object. But we can never make ourselves into 'objects' in this way. The self that really needs transformation is the pushy self that is trying to bring about the transformation by its own will and is therefore standing outside it. I recognise the distinction well. A priest in my community calls that kind of self-manipulation "screw-driver spirituality." I often have the feeling that I scarcely know another person until I have glimpsed his or her *naivety*. Nicer words, but vaguer, would be *innocence, simplicity*. That is the point where a person's life is just bubbling up into existence, and before it has been channelled by habit. (But habit tries to close even that tiny gap.) Genuine spirituality is innocent, simple, naive. We are capable of real transformation when these qualities are present. Without them we are capable only of changing one channel for another.

There is a powerful book by Chögyam Trungpa, entitled *Cutting through Spiritual Materialism,* and it has a direct bearing on our conversation. One can spend half a lifetime accumulating material goods and then make a bid for spiritual goods. The grasping attitude is the same, though the goods are different. A woman in the group says she read in the newspaper about a man who dispossessed his family and left all his wealth for Masses for his soul! He thought he could take his wealth with him by transferring it to another bank. There it would buy him exemption from the transforming fire! It is a crude version of a very ordinary temptation: to manipulate one's way to God without transformation of the whole self.

At the end of this session there are several pieces for firing. First they have to become bone dry in the sun, so we arrange them in the courtyard and notify the cocker spaniel that they are breakable. (His tail is the danger, not his mouth, for he wags it continually.) Someone said that half the pleasure in life consists in showing to others the mud-pies we have made; and that is what our pots and pieces look like now. They also look suddenly very small. Pots that look substantial indoors look tiny when they are taken outside. This is true of most of the things we keep in our houses. It is also poignantly true of children. And newly-made pots are in fact a little like children: the younger they are the more gently they have to be handled. A big man stoops down with a slightly awkward movement, to adjust his pot, and it is a gesture I have seen many fathers make towards their babies.

It is night and we have been stoking the kiln for the past two hours. Jets of flame are beginning to spurt through small crevices on every side, and the whole structure is glowing in the dark and shooting sparks into the sky from its mouth. Faces appear fleetingly like ghosts in its circle of light and disappear again into the darkness. The antiquity of the process and the ecstasy of fire make it seem like some pagan rite. The tribe is seeking to control and contain "the terrible divinity". He devours the sacrifice with ravenous mouth and rages in dread anger. They will steal his power, if they can, and bend it to their will.

Caroline, with smudged and flushed face, is expert in this kind of firing. She has prepared glazes and presided over the dipping of about thirty pots and nameless pieces. They are blackened, like herself, for they too have been dealing with fire. They are the survivors of a saw-dust firing that brought them to about 700°C. It seems astonishing that saw-dust, smouldering overnight in a dustbin, should reach this temperature; yet for pottery it is low, leaving the pieces quite brittle. I fire my own pots to 1150°C and 1280°C. These raku pieces will not be useful on the table or in the kitchen, but each one of them will possess a degree of individuality unattainable by any other method. Unlike the fire of an electric or a gas kiln, this untamed god of fire is reckless and unpredictable, and he leaves his mark for good or ill. The pots have been dipped in liquid glaze, which dries quickly, hiding their blackness (or part of it) with a white or coloured dust. These glazes will melt in the intense heat of the firing chamber, and harden permanently when the pots are removed. Two or three pots at a time will face their trial by fire. It is the Last Judgment, and the terrible divinity blasts as joyfully as he blesses.

Two bricks are removed from the side of the firing chamber and with a long tongs a pot is placed quickly inside, then a second and a third, and the bricks are put back with full speed. Now we wait for the dull thud that tells us a pot has exploded. There is rising expectation when this does not happen in the first minute. Half of these pots will shatter from thermal shock, and so each survivor will be greeted with joy. The maker of this first batch is standing close with big eyes. His familiar pots are in their agony and their fate is out of his hands, as when a child is being born.

Twenty minutes go by, while Caroline feeds blocks of wood into the kiln's mouth. Someone has remembered that frying sausages is *de rigeur* at a raku firing. They sizzle on top of the kiln, and the smell of food is not out of place in this strange rite. Caroline removes a brick from the side of the kiln and peers in. The glaze has melted. The ultimate test begins. She plunges a long tongs into the kiln's red heart and draws out a shining pot. It glows brightly in the dark like a live coal. She drops it in sawdust, because the raku formula requires carbon. Sparks leap into the air, and for a moment the pot is a ball of flame. Then it is plunged in a drum of water, where it hisses and drives up clouds of steam. Suddenly everything is silent, and the father of this pot just stands staring at the surface of the water as if expecting his new-born pot to reappear of its own accord. "Get it!" she tells him. He reaches down through the warm water and draws up a glimmering pot, speckled red and silver and black lustre. There is general ecstasy as the pot is passed from hand to hand. Its metallic hues almost make one believe that it is still in the heart of the fire. The glory of fire has been captured in dull clay.

As if to prove that such glory is a gift and not a wage, the next pot shatters on contact with the night air; and the third survives as far as the water, where a muffled explosion tells us its life is ended. Their brief existence will remind us of possible worlds, paths not taken, lives we might have lived. These ephemeral pots are purer, in their way, than the other. Nearer in essence to the fire itself, they are consumed by it and have perished with the dying of its flames, never turning to the world of time.

The maker of the speckled pot has now claimed his property; it is hidden in his hand; it has become a possession. It has died a different kind of death, like a caught trout. I have eyes only for the others, the vanished ones, but I will not be seduced by their matchless unreality.

10

Teaching and Learning

The teacher who walks in the shadow of the temple, among his followers, gives not of his wisdom but rather of his faith and his lovingness.

Gibran

"You put your right hand to your forehead, then under the breast, then to the left and right shoulders, saying at the same time, 'In the name of the Father and of the Son and of the Holy Ghost. Amen.'" I remember little from those early days, yet that superfluous piece of theory will always lie in my memory. Children are born imitators and could learn in two minutes to make the sign of the cross, but adults have to turn everything into words. Then the bridge between the words and the action becomes a new problem – and, to a child, a very puzzling one. The four-year-old beside me (all those years ago) managed to prove with a child's clarity that the theory was superfluous, for he had the theory wrong and yet could bless himself just as well as the rest of us. "You put your right hand to your forehead, then under the press…. "

Theory is pitifully useless when teaching someone to throw pots. This skill is in the whole body and not simply in the mind. When the explanations fail, there is a strong temptation to do it in the person's stead, for a teacher has to feel useful. But for the learner this is of no help at all. Some teachers just give up, then justify this by making a mystique of throwing. I know one such potter who tells people that this skill takes seven years to learn. His tone of voice, too, reinforces the feeling that they are being initiated into a secret priesthood. Certainly you cannot *teach* another to throw a pot, but there *is* something you can do. St Augustine concluded in *de Magistro* that no one teaches anyone anything, yet he is one of the greatest teachers the world has seen. The kind of learning that we are doing here at the wheel is embarrassingly visible. A student can parrot a lesson without understanding it, but nobody can make a pot without knowing how. Teaching, too, is simplified to its kernel and made visible. Perhaps the essence of teaching and learning is more visible in this dusty workshop than in any lecture hall.

Someone once said that a 'seat of learning' no more meant rows of seats on which young people sat to learn, than the old expression for a cathedral, 'the Bishop's Stool', meant a three-legged seat. If so, then anything, anywhere, can be a seat of learning – even this clay-spattered wheel. The gigantic man who is seated at it now does not have that blank and passive look that students develop after two days of lectures. (How can understanding, which is called one of our higher *activities,* cause people to look so passive?) This is a man who is used to succeeding by sheer strength of muscles and will. If I tell him that this method will not work he will not believe me, for when we are imprisoned in our own method we do not perceive it as a method at all. He has to go down the wrong road until the only thing he knows for sure is that he has gone wrong. His single-minded activism must run itself out; then he will learn by himself that he has to be *active and passive at once*; and, like a juggler, he just has to practise until he has the feel of it. He looks around at us and shrugs, preparing us for his defeat. He wants to give up now because his method has failed him. This is where sympathetic bystanders become essential teachers. We have to become, for the moment, his deeper, gentler will – since he is indicating that he is unable to find it in himself. *We must embody the very quality that will enable him to go on.* This is what makes a learning community to be more than the sum of its individuals. We are not isolated creatures, each working from his or her own resources. We are able to supply for one another at the subtlest level. The biggest mistake would be to supply for one another at the superficial level ("let me show you!") while feeling isolated at the deeper levels.

They humour him into trying with another lump of clay. This time he has more respect for it; the small lump is hidden completely in his enormous hands and he looks sideways as if listening to it. It is in there all right, expressing its will through a visible wobble. He is surrounded by confidence, even if he now has little of it yet in himself. This is the essential bridge between despair and hope, and it is at the heart of learning and teaching.

Though the lump is not centred he wants to open it up and raise it into a pot. I tell him what will happen when he does this: it will wobble itself to destruction within half a minute, for it will be heavier on one side than on the other. He is impatient to do it, nevertheless; and I explain that he is now attempting something that would defeat the most skilled potter. In pottery, as in other matters, most of our problems arise from the attempt to do something at the wrong time or under impossible conditions.

Deal with the difficult while it is still easy;
deal with the big while it is still small.
The wise one, by never dealing with great problems,
accomplishes greatness.
  Lao Tzu

Our friend has understood this and he does not really hope to make a pot at this stage, he says; he just wants to enjoy the whirling clay and to watch the way it goes out of control. Thank God for this kind of clarity, for he will experience no frustration or disappointment now – even though there will be no pot to show for his efforts. By any standard of throwing this is failure, but why should he put himself under the restraint of the word 'throwing'? Let that be for tomorrow or the next day. Besides, the best preparation for then is the freedom to play and to change definitions now. From childhood we are taught to make the present a preparation for the future. Perhaps children hold the secret: we should play more.

  The large man now yields his place at the wheel to a woman who has some experience of throwing. She centres the lump with ease, opens it and draws up the sides. She gives it belly (even the language of pottery is earthy) and draws in the neck. But somehow this pot lacks shape; it looks as though it simply ran out of clay – exhausted rather than finished. There is a mirror beside the wheel, in which you can see your pots side-on and from a distance. When she sees her pot reflected there she falls out of love with it instantly, and with one movement scrapes it off the wheel-head. There is shocked disapproval from the others, as if an innocent creature had been wantonly slaughtered. She has a good eye and no self-indulgence at all. Another pot appears just as quickly and she is sizing it up, judge and executioner in one. There is a certain slackness and lack of necessity about it; it will never pass, for it is too unlike herself. She is about to seal its fate when I suggest that she narrow its mouth a little more and then blow, or rather *breathe*, into it. She has never done this before and wants to know what size the mouth should be. "Small." This is uncannily like mouth-to-mouth resuscitation. Or it might remind one of God breathing life into Adam in the beginning. Hilariously, she wipes her lips on her sleeve. (She will have more reason to do so afterwards!) Then she puts her mouth to its mouth and breathes into it. It raises and stretches itself like a living being. Where there was only a flaccid shape before, there is a vital pot, full of energy. She gives a little scream of delight when she sees it; a real pot has come into existence. Carefully she runs a wire under it and lifts it off the wheel-head. When it is safely on the shelf she relaxes and bursts into delighted laughter. We were born to experience moments like this.

Several others try their luck on the wheel, but this one woman's success has created a vacuum behind it. They want to imitate what she did. It seems we always want to milk God for something other than what we are getting.

The dark man near the door shifts forward and begins to talk. He has the black look and the too fluent speech that teachers often develop. I can see him in control of a tough class. He has picked up the only book in the place, the pottery log-book with its spattered cover, and is holding it in his hand without looking at it. Oddly I have never thought of it as a book till this moment. He asks about glazes: content, method of application, colours, melting point, and so on. When I mention lead as a fluxing agent he says this is dangerous and asks whether there are any controls on the use of it by potters. Cadmium is much more poisonous than lead, I assure him. (Big problems put little ones in their place.) But we'll come to that later. Meanwhile would he like to try the wheel? He shifts himself around uncomfortably. He has lost his teacher's manner for the moment. Sensing this, the others urge him on and almost push him towards the wheel. He is one of the boys now, and all the better for it. What a disaster when a teacher is only a teacher! The one essential thing he has to teach is how to learn. But how can he teach this if he is not a learner himself? He will give his students the dry bones of knowledge.

He sits at the wheel and asks multiple, dove-tailing questions, but they are only a cover for inaction. To ask questions is not the same as being a learner. Questions and answers are worthless here, I assure him. He settles himself uncertainly to the task. I know what it is like to be taken on one's weak side. It is like those almost impossible things that children challenge you to do, like wiggling one's ears or moving one finger without moving its neighbours. The wobbling clay must seem to him like the youngster who cannot keep quiet. His face is dark again with disapproval. It is probably not a new experience for him to find a creature that is perfectly vulnerable and yet not subject to his will. Students develop this art of blending servility and defiance in perfect measure; it is their way of surviving; they have the wisdom of clay. He exerts such overpowering force that the lump detaches itself from the wheel-head. He slaps it back, but by now the surfaces have become wet, so that the lump floats freely and pointlessly on the wheel-head, trapped between his hands. He has dominated it, but to no purpose. I suggest to him that he try with a new lump, but he says he has had enough and walks away from the wheel with a dismissive gesture. I can imagine only too vividly what this scowling man does to his unlucky students.

His bad grace and lack of humour have cast a gloom on us, and I feel an urgent need to rescue myself from it. Even the group clown has gone into himself. Yet who knows whether this mood might not have something to teach us too?

"You would have to be a very disciplined person to learn throwing," someone remarks; and our teacher darkens even more, for discipline is his speciality. Hitherto, throwing had been pure fun; now we are talking about discipline. Very well then; what is discipline? The word itself tells you: *it is the process of learning.* It does not mean conformity, suppression, repetition, imitation – though in our dullness we often reduce it to this. So I do not discipline myself and then learn; learning is its own discipline. For example, throwing is not the result of discipline; it *is* a discipline. It is a continual learning, an attention and a sensitivity to this lump of clay now – not a headful of dead information to be reproduced at will and to which I must conform my mind and my actions.

The test of genuine teaching is whether in the long haul the teacher has influenced the student to pay real spontaneous attention to the realities of life, for only realities deserve our attention. I have met hundreds of educated people who are spectacularly indifferent to real things and situations, and seem capable of no more than repetition: if they see something they have seen before, or have read about, they recognise it; otherwise it remains invisible to them. They live out of their memories and allow their native intelligence to atrophy. Their education has inducted them into what Swift called "the tribes of Answerers, Considerers, Observers, Reflectors, Detectors, Remarkers." How many people would look at the Mona Lisa if they had not been told that it was the thing to do? (Once when it was removed from its position, a greater number of people came to see its empty place than ever came, in an equal period, to see the painting itself.) I feel a sudden resentment against the several miscast teachers I have had in my life, and against many others I have seen in action. I must be careful not to project it all on this one man. Argument with him would be futile; it would make his hardness harder still. I must think myself into his fears and limitations, and act kindly towards him, while not going along with any of his routines. Nor will I be alone: the place, the clay, the company will also be at work to soften his spirit. We must embody gentleness for him, since he has lost touch with his own gentleness. Perhaps this is what he is searching for. After all he must be searching for something; otherwise he would not be here.

Now comes a sprightly one, thank God, but needing all the same to be pushed forward by her friends. This little charade is probably a shield against appearing too confident; it is needed because of the certain failure ahead. *Kluger Mann baut vor* – show us that it is not your idea at all, so that when you fail it will not really be your failure; on the contrary, it will show how right you were in not wanting to come forward! She has an open face and a merry laugh, and she checks everyone's face once a minute to make sure we are all friends.

She asks if I would centre the clay for her, because she wants to make a pot. She begins to open the centred lump, but loses nerve a little and lets her hands travel with the clay. "Stay at the three o'clock position!" – she has slipped a quarter of the circle. In the East, potters tend to spin their wheel clockwise and work at the nine o'clock position. How inconceivable it seems! Yet one arrangement is as good as the other. However, twelve o'clock is a different story: at twelve o'clock you have little control of what happens, because one hand is eclipsing the other. The spinning clay seems to mesmerise her and she keeps following it rather than anchoring at the three o'clock position. When you touch the spinning clay at one point you are touching it all around, so there is no need to move. But when everything in sight is spinning it is hard to stand still yourself and not be drawn into its swell. She is not clear on what she should be doing, and this is what is mesmerising her; her head is spinning along with the clay. "Do nothing to the clay now," I tell her, "just let it flow through your hands, as if you had dipped them in a stream." This languid image succeeds immediately in settling her. "Now begin to squeeze slightly." Every action on the spinning clay has to be performed like a ritual, at a measured pace, for the practical reason that it has to be given time to do the full circle; jerky movements unbalance a pot.

We are all waiting for visible results, but nothing changes at all as the minutes go by. No matter what the medium, it takes a long time to learn how to be gentle and strong at the same time. Gentleness can fade to a helpless passivity, strength can become brute force. I have found no better school than wheel-work for teaching me the life-long art of identifying, distinguishing and balancing these. There are many false appearances of activity: the man running to the pubs or forever pursuing females is not active but *passive;* he is driven by instincts that he has given himself up to. His life may seem to be a frenzy of activity but it is not activity at all. He is not acting from his full self or out of his real identity; he is being driven by an impersonal force, like a newspaper driven along the street by the wind. Our young friend looks passive now, but she is not more passive than when she was moving frantically and making little screams of dismay as the clay pulled her after it.

There was once a wise man who was sitting in his house with his disciples when a little bird flew in through the open window. The disciples jumped up and tried with much noise and waving of their arms to frighten it towards the window. But the harder they tried the more panicked and blind the bird became. Finally the wise man told them to sit down. Little by little the bird became quieter too, and would change its perch enquiringly from time to time. Once when it perched near the open window the wise man clapped his hands and the bird flew straight to freedom.

I wish we had the wisdom of that wise man to shift the girl from this impasse. "Do something!" says one of her friends suddenly, a wise one, I hope. She squeezes the clay, and gives a shout of delight when she sees it rising. A rising shape only *seems* to defy the law of gravity. It rises under pressure. If you block all the easier routes, while maintaining the pressure, it has to go up. It does nothing by itself except spin: that is, it distributes your touch throughout the full circle of itself. You have to give it very clear directions, because every ambiguity will be made instantly visible in the round. It is a remorseless mirror to your action: every twitch is magnified. The clay walls rise uncertainly and she loses her nerve, makes a sudden, aimless movement, and the whole subsides without a whisper. There is nothing so definitive as the collapse of a pot.

Does the clay say to its fashioner, 'What are you making?' Does
the thing shaped say, 'You have no skill?' (Isaiah 45:9)

Isaiah was a great prophet, but no potter. Pots have hundred of ways
of saying "You have no skill" and "What are you making?" Besides,
they speak a language that he would have understood: symbolic action.

This particular pot has certainly spoken to our young friend. She has
enjoyed the making and the unmaking of it, she says, and would like
to practise later. She needs to practise and practise, she says. There is an
image that stays in my mind: an old golfer in Cork called 'the Master',
watching some players from the window and saying, half to himself,
"There they go, practising their faults!"

I learned from a wise man, I tell her, that you should never practise.
Learning is always new.

11

Dancing and Stillness

I find it … a reassuring thought, in these morose times, that at
any given moment a sizable portion of the human race is dancing.
  – W. Anderson

If we are to believe the physicists, solid objects are not solid; they are
pure energy, and all reality is a dance. Solid objects are universally out
of favour, it seems; the Age of Aquarius has dawned over every field.

How is it possible to speak about anything if nothing stands still? But
this predicament brings its own kind of blessing. We have lost so many
securities that we are able to see a truth we could not have seen before:
that words obscure more effectively when they are fixed than when they
move. We lack a stable culture that would continue to give life to fixed
words. When our words become fixed they die, and their dead bodies
obscure the truth. It is our burden to live in times when the dearest words,
such as *God, faith, love, truth,* will not stay in place, will not stay still.

We could hold tight and insist that the world is what we have always
taken it to be, but we have been advised against it by many wise people.
T. S. Eliot affirmed that the sound tree would put forth new leaves; there
is no need to gum the old ones on the branches. Instead of preserving
leaves we should try to stimulate the life that produced them. It is foolish,
he said, to associate tradition with the immovable. Fidelity to tradition
does not mean " … following the ways of the immediate generation
before us in a blind and timid adherence to its successes…. Tradition is
a matter of much wider significance. It cannot be inherited and if you
want it you must obtain it by great labour."

The *labour* that dance-meditation requires is plain for all to see – or as plain as the dimly-lit meditation room will allow. And no one could call these twenty people *immovable*. The sedate Eliot would shudder perhaps at being asked to patronise these sweaty proceedings. But we are doing our best, according to our lights, to stimulate the life within us and put forth new leaves.

Sometimes a mental or a spiritual immobility is best cured through the body. In the thirteenth century, Aquinas battled against odds to defend his teaching on the 'unicity of form'. It was not popular then to say that it is the same soul in us that grows our toe nails and that contemplates the Divine Essence. To this day the consequences of this teaching have not been fully accepted; it is more convenient to partition life into several areas than to believe that the human person is an inviolable unity. We are attempting in this dance-meditation to allow the whole person to dance.

Almost as soon as we hear the words 'free dance', a host of inhibitions emerges to overpower most of us and root us to the spot. The self-critic in us – that intimate crippler who is yet not intimate at all but public – disowns us and stands by the wall, immobilising us with its looks. Our ambition is to get this boring creature to dance.

IT IS NIGHT and the meditation room is dimly lit, to encourage the timid. We sit in a circle in silence. It is right to begin out of silence: then there is less danger of carrying through with the usual bustle. We are to dance for integrity, not for beauty; for the self and God, not for others. So we allow no spectators. We are in the age of spectators, bystanders, commentators, critics. To be a spectator is to be involved only passively, on one's own terms and without risks. Spectators are given an inexplicable authority; so the self-critic within each dancer would identify instantly with the spectators by the wall, and we would see ourselves only through their eyes. This is seldom a gift from God, as Robbie Burns thought, but the curse of self-consciousness, the replacement of the real self with a divided self – the birth of ego.

The story is older than us. King David "danced before the Lord with all his might." His wife, who had been watching from a window, saw him "leaping and dancing before the Lord." When he came home she said:

> "What a fine reputation the king of Israel has won himself today
> … displaying himself under the eyes of his servants' maids, as any
> buffoon might display himself. David answered, 'I was dancing
> for the Lord, not for them'" (2 Samuel 6).

Here tonight we are going to attempt to move in meditation: that is, to move wholly, with undivided mind. In Christian circles, meditation has too often been identified with motionlessness. In Zen there is a meditative walking known as *kinhin,* and indeed an awareness that all actions can be a form of meditation. I used to use a form of dance-meditation devised by an Indian guru, but I abandoned it long since in favour of home produce. In most religions, dance has been used as a form of prayer, but it is surprisingly rare in the Christian faith. Yet why should we not move the whole body in prayer? What is so special about the tongue or the brain waves that we should consider them sufficient by themselves? It is very easy for these to fake, but the body never lies.

We remove shoes and socks and take up our positions, some with arms self-consciously straight, all facing outwards (a further concession to the timid). I have chosen music that has little interest except its rhythm. The instruction is to move the whole body as if one were being dangled at the end of a string attached to the top of the head. This is a time to discover how closely akin we have become to the beasts of burden. There is a lot of mechanical thumping of the ground nearby; the Spirit of Gravity is doing a clog-dance on my left. That is not a problem, for eventually the big man will become bored with this kind of movement and will go on to something else.

This is the secret: the dance goes on and on past the threshold of boredom. We have to go beyond that threshold if we are to discover genuinely new things. Tiredness is a great help: with tiredness comes a certain economy of effort, the thumping and twitching grow less, and there is a new flowing quality in the movement.

Men have taken the rigidity of the machine as their model of how they should move and act. Teenage boys, and even grown men, often reproduce the rigid gait of the tough guy they have admired in films. It is all imitation and searching for a self-image. The saddle-sore John Wayne was no less a model than was Twiggy in her day. I have been told that there is no physiological reason – even granting the difference in hip structure – why men and women should walk so differently. It is mainly a learned difference. In this, as in everything else, the body is manifesting the mind. One evil result (for men and women alike) is that many men can only express themselves roughly or violently when it comes to the body.

However, the big man on my left may be escaping under cover of darkness from this masculine bondage. I should not look, but I cannot help being aware, that he is beginning to move in a less halting way, with a certain grace at times. Even his hips are moving. The stereotypes would allow this privilege only to women. But I cannot imagine him moving like this at a staff dance. Many men try to reassure themselves of their own masculinity by imposing the rigid stereotype on one another. It is comical to see the different images passing by in succession: sometimes he falls away from being a dancer and begins a rolling shuffle like a heavyweight limbering up in the ring before a fight; for a while he resembles a goalkeeper waiting for a penalty kick; then he does an impression of disco that would surely send his teenage children rolling on the floor.

It is as hard to do one's own kind of movement as it is to hum an original tune without slipping into some beaten track. It is like working with clay and trying to make something that has no name. This kind of dance is not expressive, if by 'expressive' we mean that it conveys some pre-selected emotion or concept. It is free of 'products', like our earlier work with clay. It is about unity and freedom within the self, and not about portrayal or imitation. If we ever move like this it is usually for no more than a few seconds. But this sustained primitive movement is a powerful corrective to living in the head.

Now the music changes to a more flowing rhythm, and we feel free to dance around the room rather than stay in one place. Do not put will-power and deliberation into it, I told them earlier – an instruction that has some odd contradiction in it. An image is better: imagine that you are a curtain blowing in the breeze. Imagine the music to be the breeze. We float around like dancing dervishes, with a freedom that could not have been imagined before.

> Everything flows and nothing abides,
> everything gives way and nothing stands fixed.
> – Heraclitus

Though it is random movement, there is scarcely ever a collision – an surprising fact in itself. It is rigidity, not freedom, that causes collisions. Gradually the movement begins to flow in a current, like water in a sink. It is nearly always anti-clockwise, I notice. (Would it go the other way in Australia?)

But I should not be watching my neighbours, even covertly. This is for oneself. I want to discover anew what the word 'God' means. It was not the *word* 'God' that moved the saints, but the mysterious reality to which it pointed.

Like everyone else I have bad memories of the word 'God': as a teenager I associated it with callous teachers, with two or three people who were overbearing when they were not indifferent, with church-yard yew trees that looked so sad and different from other trees. It was not the clergy or any of their institutions, but gentle parents, who kept God in trust for me and were channels of the tradition.

Martin Buber called the word 'God' the most heavy-laden of all words:

> None has become so soiled, so mutilated. Generations … have laid the burden of their anxious lives upon this word and weighed it to the ground; it lies in the dust and bears their whole burden.

Can God rise from so much death? And if so, how will God be called?

> If I took the purest, most sparkling concept from the inner treasure-chamber of the philosophers, I could only capture thereby an unbinding product of thought. I could not capture the presence of

him whom the generations ... have honoured and degraded with their awesome living and dying.

If I am to glimpse God it must be out of these eyes of mine. I must bring my heavy past to such a buoyancy that it will dance before the Lord. I must drink the cup of my own life and not reject a single drop. In a beautiful book on Sufi mysticism, called *The Whirling Dervishes,* Ira Friedlander wrote:

> Wise people are called 'balakesh', meaning 'One who took the draught of all difficulties.' The difficulties of life were regarded as a wine that, once drunk, would disappear.

Enemies engage the mind more intensely than friends do; and so hurts, resentments, abuses, vexations can become the very stuff of my inner life and weigh me to the ground. The way to turn enemies into friends is to embrace them: I must embrace my past, receive and feel its hurts, resist the urge to reconstruct it as fiction. Then I begin to be free of its burden. If this must take place in the individual, must it not also take place in the whole culture? We must embrace the past if it is not to remain a dead weight around our necks. When we do, it is transformed into ourselves; it becomes our own flesh.

This is the most radical change. It is the difference between life and death: the dead past becoming alive in the present. God is God of the present, whose name was revealed on the mountain as 'I am', not 'I was'. But if we refuse any of the past it becomes dead words in our mouths and washed-out feelings in our hearts. And if the past *is forced* on the present without being transformed into it, then God is very distant – God will be like the young man who leapt away at the taking of Christ and left his cloak in their hands.

We flow around the meditation room, an intermingling tide of move-ment. There is great joy in everything wholehearted, but only drudgery when the self is divided. While I am dancing I think I will never again talk but only dance to God. It is a full and joyful manifestation of one's whole being. There is no room for distractions. When we are distracted at prayer, it does not mean that we are 'invaded' by distractions; on the contrary, they are welcome guests. The idle parts of our being need something to do, and they invite them in. They suck them in by vacuum. Nor is there any need to force certain feelings, when one dances. There is nothing quite so false as false feelings, since they pretend to come from a deeper place than words. It is wrong to force them and wrong to avoid them. They flow by themselves when one is fully alive.

I have friends who drag themselves through half-hours of meditation every day, struggling to stay awake and to keep distractions at bay. What a liberation it would be for them to dance to the Lord instead – even once! It would also introduce a life-giving truthfulness into prayer, for the body cannot tell a lie, even to God (who is more accustomed than anyone else to hearing them).

I picture a mountain stream dancing down between the stones. There is music, light and life in it. But one gallon of the water loses its nerve and wants security instead of this dizzying swirl. So it pours itself out to the side, becoming a small pool. Now it has security, a tiny coastline, a narrow identity. But as the weeks go by it becomes aware that it is only a stagnant puddle. It tried to save its life but lost it. After much stagnation and despair it pours itself back into the stream, imagining that all is now lost; it loses its familiar coastline, the identity it had chosen out of fear. But instead, life suddenly starts for it again, and music and the dance. In losing its life it gained life.

As the movement continues I become aware that at the heart of it there is a kind of stillness that is different from the stillness of fixity: it is deeper and more alive. To move from this centre is to experience an astonishing buoyancy and exuberance. No doubt God can reach us just as well in times of mediocrity and boredom, but if God could not reach us in moments of depth and exuberance God would be a poor God. It is a stillness in the midst of activity, so it is able to carry over into the turbulence of ordinary life.

In turbulent times St Ambrose gave this advice to the Christians of Milan:

There may be a storm at sea, but a fish swims; it is not drowned, because it is used to swimming. For you this world is a sea. It has all kinds of waves and currents and fierce tempests. You too must be a fish, so that the world's waves do not swallow you up.

I used to feel uneasy about the many rigid images of God in the Scriptures: *rock, fortress, shield, stronghold, warrior.* They seemed to express such insecurity on our part. The little girl from the broken home always wept when they sang "Rock of Ages". What we lack we long for; when we feel insecure we long for security.

I got over my unease, once for all, during dance-meditation a few years ago. A distinction became clear: between *fixity* and *fidelity*. Images of the one are easily misinterpreted as images of the other. If, in our insecurity, we have a leaning towards psychological fixity we will not be content with a faithful God, we will long for a God who never moves at all – and for an unmoving theology and spirituality. This psychological fixity often appears as an addiction to *certainty*, an addiction that the real world does little to satisfy; so it has to be satisfied from the mind itself. If we are looking for certainty we will inevitably close our eyes. In my own search for God, it was good to rediscover that the mediaeval theologians described God as "pure act." This made me fall in love with some of them again, like long-lost cousins. And when Aquinas asked himself whether God was perfect (meaning, literally, 'completely made or finished') he quoted St Gregory: "Stammering, we echo the heights of God as best we can," and said that the word 'perfect' (like all other words) is stretched beyond all finite contexts when it is used of God. Here was no fixity but a profound awareness of God's transcendence. God is absolute, and the word 'absolute' means 'unfettered', 'unfixed'. However, there is a metaphor from St Catherine of Siena that, for me, surpasses all others in vividness even if not in precision; and it comes particularly alive at this dance-meditation:

> The soul is in God and God is in the soul as the fish is in the ocean and the ocean is in the fish.

There was once a fish who heard tell of the ocean and set out to find it, seeking directions of every fish he met as he swam. He was unaware that he was swimming in the ocean, and so he could not find it anywhere. God is the nearest thing to me, and is therefore hard to find. The ocean passes through the fish's gills, with life-giving oxygen; the Spirit of God lives in my being, animating me from within.

The dancing is over now, the music has stopped, and we are sitting in silence again. The whole body is hot and alive. Stagnant energy has been danced out, and a fresh energy begins to pool within. There is a crystallisation of one's being, and God seems very near.

Twenty years ago someone said that we may have to meet God in the dance before we can define God in the doctrine. We convert everything too quickly into words. I suspect that God is less interested in these than I had imagined. If words do not reflect an experience of God they are only chaff, with no seed of life in them.

One of Herman Hesse's characters, a musician, said: "There is no point at all in talking about music. I never talk about music…. You see, I am a musician, not a professor." And Renoir felt the same way about his own art: "I am getting tired of my friends; they are always talking about painting and there is nothing to be said about painting." The deepest Christians have known that the supreme art of knowing God requires no less silence. The much used word 'mystic' comes from the Greek '*muein*': 'to be silent'. Justin Martyr said:

> No-one can give a name to God, who is too great for words; if anyone dares to say that it is possible to do so, they must be suffering from an incurable madness.

If I hold my tongue for a while the rest of my being may come to life (perhaps with much perspiration, as in this dance) and it will listen for God. Though properly God has no name, multitudes of names have been used by people whose lives were immersed in God. Pascal spoke of *Fire,* countless others said *Spirit* others again *Fountain of living water:* but no one has called God *Earth.* The three moving elements are able to stammer something about God's vitality, but gravity and fixity we hug to ourselves.

❧❧

"A GREETING built a village," said some wise African. Within hours of greeting one another last week we had become a community. Now it is time to douse the fire and move on. But a village, thank God, can survive many goodbyes.